BELLINI'S FEAST OF THE GODS

BELLINI'S FEAST OF THE GODS

A STUDY IN VENETIAN HUMANISM

BY EDGAR WIND

Published for the Harvard College Library
by Harvard University Press
Cambridge, Massachusetts
1948

To M.W.

LONDON : GEOFFREY CUMBERLEGE
OXFORD UNIVERSITY PRESS

PREFACE

THE plan to publish a short series of studies on Venetian humanism originated in two seminars which were held in 1945 and 1947 at the Houghton Library at Harvard University, under the auspices of the Department of Printing and Graphic Arts. The subject of these discussions – *The Dream of Poliphilus* and *Titian and Pietro Aretino* – will be presented in two subsequent studies. The present essay, which is based on a lecture delivered at the National Gallery of Art, is inseparable from the others both in theme and method, and is here included with the consent of the National Gallery.

In a study of this kind, it is impossible to uphold the boundaries between art and literature; the subject demands that we trespass. While it may be natural for a library to be tolerant of this offence, a prejudice in favor of books is generally suspect among connoisseurs; it smacks of that 'literary approach to art' of which we have been happily cured by a militant generation. But I fear that literature behaves very much like Horace's Nature: it returns even if you drive it out with a pitchfork. It would be far more convenient if art were pure. A literary allusion obstructs our vision – until it is understood.

The footnotes to this essay may be ignored by readers who trust my argument on sight, but I am confident that there will be few of these. And as I hope that there may be some who would wish to pursue the subject further, I have made the references sufficiently critical and explicit to spare them some of my own trouble.

The help I have received cannot be matched by adequate thanks. I am indebted first and foremost to the director and staff of the Houghton Library, in particular to Philip Hofer, who planned the publication of this essay and nursed it into print. His assistant, Dr. Weinberger, has helped me over many a bibliographical hurdle. For generous aid in obtaining books and photographs, I am indebted to the officers of the Harvard College Library, the Library of Congress, the William Allan Neilson Library at Smith College, the Yale University Library, the Warburg Institute, the Fogg Museum of Art, the John G. Johnson Collection, the Metropolitan Museum of Art, the Museum of Fine Arts in Boston, the National Gallery of Art, the Louvre, and the Musée Condé. I have greatly benefited by the advice of Oliver Larkin and Jean Seznec. If some of my sentences are shorter or more fluent than they would be otherwise, this is due to the skill and charity of William M. Ivins, Jr., to whom I must apologize for the flaws which still remain. The manuscript was read also by John Walker, whose interest spurred me on to publication.

As the terms of the William Allan Neilson professorship have enabled me to pursue these and other studies undisturbed, I hope that the president and the trustees of Smith College will regard this little book as an expression of my gratitude.

E. W.

Northampton, Massachusetts
20 February 1948

CONTENTS

At Lampsacus, your chosen house,
Priapus, in your love,
I dedicate, I consecrate
By your good leave this grove:
Because a mighty cult is yours
In all the towns that are
By Hellespont, that shore of shores
Most oysterish, by far.

CATULLUS
translated by Sir William Marris

BELLINI'S FEAST OF THE GODS

Facetious Painting in Isabella d'Este's Grotta

AS might be expected of a learned princess, Isabella d'Este's patronage of art was dictatorial, fanciful, and pedantic. She ordered pictures for the sake of "ideas," and insisted that her instructions be followed precisely. That her conduct was as vigorous as her taste is all too amply proved by her letters. Yet, in accusing her of a complete absence of artistic tact, some of her critics have perhaps been unduly swayed by their own aesthetic sensibilities; for it is obvious that not all of her artists found her erudition distasteful. Perugino, it is true, was out of his depth when he tried to cope with one of her learned programs; but under precisely the same conditions Mantegna produced two of his greatest works, as did also Correggio; while Costa's modest but conscientious talents proved quite adaptable to her wishes. Apparently, she required a "learned style" of her painters, an intricate manner, minutely labored, and she would not tolerate an unlettered caprice: "You are not to add anything of your own," she imperiously ended her instructions to Perugino for *The Battle of Love and Chastity*.[1]

To disregard this kind of categorical prohibition is not necessarily a sign of artistic strength. A Perugino might find these restrictions stifling, but the constraint seems to have suited Mantegna. And even at its worst, Isabella's terse manner of telling an artist exactly what she wanted him to paint could have a beneficial effect; for if she did not persuade the painter,

[1] W. Braghirolli, "Notizie e Documenti inediti intorno a Pietro Vannucci detto il Perugino," *Giornale di Erudizione Artistica*, II, 1873, p. 163–166.

she was bound to provoke him, and the provocation might set off a creative process in a direction unforeseen, and perhaps undesired, by the determined and bewildered patroness.

This proved to be her experience with Giovanni Bellini. He baffled Isabella by his evasions, at one time enraging her to such an extent that she thought of invoking the law against him; for he found her payment far more readily acceptable than her program, and while consistently refusing to adopt the one, seemed disinclined to relinquish the other. The crux of the matter was that she desired from Bellini a "pagan fantasy" to match Mantegna's paintings in the study room of her famous Grotta in the Corte Vecchia,[2] an apartment to be decorated as a poetic retreat, in which the study of ancient authors might be associated with an escape into Arcadia.[3] In trying to interest Bellini in this task she miscalculated the effects of her strategy. She had assumed that the prospect of competing with his brother-in-law, Mantegna, would be an incentive to Bellini, and so it was; but she did not consider that this might at the same time deter him from attempting a "pagan fantasy" – a type of painting in which Mantegna was an expert and he himself inexperienced. For four years (1501 to 1504) Isabella's agents in Venice, Lorenzo da Pavia and Michele Vianello, made a series of futile attempts, on the one hand to convince Isabella that pagan fables of an argumentative kind were not in Bellini's style, and on the other hand to persuade Bellini to carry out a commitment to which he

[2] C. Yriarte's attempt to assign the Grotta three successive locations ("Isabella d'Este et les Artistes de son Temps," *Gazette des Beaux-Arts*, XIII–XV, 1895–1896) has been refuted by Mantuan archivists. Cf. A. Luzio, "I Ritratti d'Isabella d'Este," *Emporium*, XI, 1900, p. 344ff.; also the summary in P. Kristeller, *Andrea Mantegna* (English ed.), 1901, p. 346. For conclusive evidence that the Grotta remained on the ground floor of the Corte Vecchia, see Raffaello Toscano's poem *L'Edificatione di Mantova*, Padua, 1586: "In Corte vecchia è giù posto a terreno/Quel loco, che la Grotta il Mondo appella," etc. A more general description in Leandro Alberti, *Descrittione di Tutta Italia*, 1550, fol. 353 v, also in G. G. Trissino, *I Ritratti*, 1549.

[3] The decoration of the vault in Correggio's *Camera di S. Paolo* (fig. 32) may derive from the Grotta in Mantua. There is a similar arbor in Mantegna's *Madonna della Vittoria* (fig. 31), a picture which was designed according to Isabella's instructions. On Correggio's own paintings for her Grotta, see below, p. 52ff.

was in honor bound. Neither party would yield, and Isabella's mortification reached its height when, after having hoped in vain for Bellini's surrender, she received from the far more pliant Perugino a picture which proved "inaccurate."

"I really do not know," she wrote to Paride da Ceresara, her humanist adviser in "inventing" these programs, "which of us two suffers the most from the interminable delays of these painters – I who see no end to the decoration of my Camerino, and you who are every day required to supply new compositions, which these wayward masters either refuse to execute or else render inaccurately." [4] In the end, she compromised with Bellini, who painted for her a *Nativity* – produced (as her agents took care to inform her) "with great pains, from a sense of honor, and particularly because of Mantegna." [5] She placed it in her bedroom.

But the incident rankled in her mind, and presumably in Bellini's too. So when Pietro Bembo paid her a visit (1505) and she showed him her Camerino, she could not resist telling him of her disappointment in his friend and compatriot, Bellini. Thereupon Bembo himself offered to resume the negotiations in Venice, and carried them out with such success that they resulted (as we propose to prove in this essay) in Bellini's painting *The Feast of the Gods* (fig. 1).

Admittedly, the *Feast of the Gods* holds a unique position among Bellini's works. Completed when he was about eighty years old,[6] this is one of his very rare pictures of pagan gods.[7] In it he made them look rather

[4] J. Cartwright, *Isabella d'Este*, I, 1904, p. 372; Yriarte, *op. cit.*, *Gazette des Beaux-Arts*, XV, 1896, p. 331.

[5] Braghirolli, "Carteggio di Isabella d'Este Gonzaga intorno ad un quadro di Giambellino," *Archivio Veneto*, XIII, ii, 1877, p. 370–383, comprising nineteen letters written between 5 March 1501 and 9 July 1504.

[6] Semi-miraculous in itself, Bellini's "old age" is further complicated by the following footnote in Morelli: "The late Signor Cecchetti discovered a curious document (published in the *Archivio Veneto*, XXXIV, 204), according to which the widow of Giovanni Bellini made her will in 1554, thirty-eight years, therefore, after the death of her husband, who died at the age of eighty-eight" ("The Borghese and Doria-Pamfili Galleries in Rome," *Italian Painters*, I, 1900, p. 269, n. 2).

[7] Three other pagan pictures have been attributed to him (*Orpheus*, Na-

odd, half-elegant, half-boorish, and decidedly un-Olympian. Were it not for some unmistakable attributes – such as the staff of Mercury, the trident of Neptune, the wreath of wheat in Ceres' hair, or the ass attended by Silenus – one might take this to be a company of rustics, drowsily enjoying a *fête champêtre*. Some of the gods are a little ill-mannered, others appear to be tipsy. Apollo, distinguished by two unbecomingly foreshortened legs (but otherwise recognizable by his laurel wreath and the *lira da braccio* which he holds clumsily behind the legs of his neighbor),[8] has such difficulties in lifting his cup to his mouth that he is charitably assisted by Ceres, who herself is rather disheveled (fig. 6). Even Jupiter looks awkward, with his tumbler almost touching his nose, and his eagle so bedraggled a fowl that it could be mistaken for a black goose (fig. 2). Among the best-behaved characters are the servants, the satyrs and nymphs carrying the food and drink, and a Pan playing a flute. Yet the two caryatid-like nymphs are suspiciously stiff; and their garments are less stately than their postures: one "through her ripped robe reveals her breast; another bares her shoulder" [9] (fig. 4).

But if the subject is exceptional in Bellini's art, this eccentric representation of the pagan gods is not at all unique in its kind. It belongs to a literary and pictorial genre particularly dear to Renaissance humanists, who knew that the ancients themselves had treated their sacred subjects with irony. The Homeric poems offered models of the facetious as well as of

tional Gallery, Washington; *Venus with a Mirror*, Museum, Vienna; *Infant Bacchus*, Duveen Brothers, New York, formerly Benson Collection, London), but all of these are questionable. His few unquestionable pagan designs (like the sacrificial scenes in the background of *The Redeemer*, National Gallery, London, or the little panels for a mirror in the Academy, Venice) are either moral or allegorical images and hence belong to a different category from the *Feast of the Gods*. A drawing of a pagan sacrifice in the Fogg Museum (Loeser Bequest), published as a Bellini by D. von Hadeln, *Venezianische Zeichnungen des Quattrocento*, 1925, pl. 67, is hardly by his hand. See A. Mongan and P. J. Sachs, *Drawings in the Fogg Museum of Art*, I, 1940, p. 19, no. 25; H. Tietze and E. Tietze-Conrat, *The Drawings of the Venetian Painters*, 1944, p. 83, A292.

[8] E. Winternitz, "A Lira da Braccio in Giovanni Bellini's Feast of the Gods," *Art Bulletin*, XXVIII, 1946, p. 114f.

[9] Ovid, *Fasti*, I, 408–409 (Sir James Frazer's translation, with commentary, 1929).

the heroic style; and so did Ovid and Apuleius.[10] In the contest between Democritus and Heraclitus, the tragedian Seneca gave the crown to laughter.[11] The wide acceptance of this lesson during the Renaissance is proved by the enthusiastic revival of Lucian.[12] To laugh at the pagan gods with understanding became a sign of humanist grace, which was transmitted from poets to painters. Thus Erasmus' *Praise of Folly* was illustrated by Holbein with marginal drawings containing travesties of classical myths: Jupiter spanking Ate, or giving painful birth to Minerva while Vulcan, his midwife, assists with an axe.[13] Thomas More, like Erasmus, wrote imitations of Lucian, and a very competent parody of this kind was produced also by Pirckheimer, Albrecht Dürer's ponderous friend.[14] The particular bent of Dürer's own sense of humor has been a matter of debate,[15] but there can be no question that Mantegna, whom he admired, was accessible to Homeric laughter. In one of his paintings for the Grotta of Isabella d'Este — the very room for which Bellini was to

[10] E. K. Rand, *Ovid and his Influence*, 1925, p. 73. H. Fränkel, *Ovid: A Poet between two Worlds*, 1945, p. 239, n. 6. E. H. Haight, *Apuleius and his Influence*, 1927, p. 111–123, with particular reference to Poggio and his *Facetiae* (p. 113).

[11] Seneca, *De Tranquillitate Animae* 15, 2; *De Ira* II, 10, 5. See also Juvenal, *Satires* X, 28, and Lucian, *On Sacrifices* 15.

[12] R. Förster, *Lucian in der Renaissance*, 1886. On the affinities between Lucian and Apuleius see Poggio's preface to his translation of Lucian's *Ass* (*Poggii Florentini Opera*, 1538, p. 138).

[13] *Encomium Moriae, i.e. Stultitae Laus*, 1515 (facsimile edition with the marginal drawings of Hans Holbein, intr. H. A. Schmid, tr. H. H. Tanzer, 1931). F. Saxl, "Holbein's Illustrations to *The Praise of Folly* by Erasmus," *The Burlington Magazine*, LXXXIII, 1943, p. 275–279, compares these drawings with the *Feast of the Gods* and adds early examples of mocking representations of pagan figures. See also *Bibliography on the Survival of the Classics*, ed. H. Meier, R. Newald, E. Wind, I, 1934, p. 211 f., no. 862.

[14] *The Praise of the Gout, or, the Gouts Apologie . . . written first in the Latine tongue by . . . B. Pirkheimerus . . . and now Englished by W. Est*, 1617. The original, *Podagrae Laus*, in: *Luciani . . . Libellus de non credendo Calumniae*, 1529. For Erasmus and More, see *Luciani . . . Opuscula . . . ab Erasmo Roterodamo et Thoma Moro . . . in Latinorum linguam traducta . . . cum declamatione Erasmica . . . Declamatio Mori* . . . 1506.

[15] I have suggested elsewhere that Dürer was joking in the style of Lucian when he represented Hercules in a Gallic outfit, and Orpheus with a derogatory inscription, a fig tree half-plucked, and a fleeing child ("'Hercules' and 'Orpheus': two Mock-Heroic Designs by Dürer," *Journal of the Warburg Institute*, II, 1939, p. 206–218). For the contrary view see E. Panofsky, *Albrecht Dürer*, 1943, I, p. 74–76, also p. 32; II, p. 26, 95.

supply a "pagan fantasy" – Mantegna actually abandoned the heroic diction and tried his hand at the facetious style. Incompatible though this may seem with his proverbial fierceness, the so-called *Parnassus* of Mantegna is conceived in that mocking spirit which Bellini exhibited in the *Feast of the Gods.* And since there are reasons for suspecting that Bellini's painting was originally designed as a rejoinder to the *Parnassus*, it is perhaps well, in reconstructing its subject, to examine Mantegna's painting first.

The Parnassus of Mantegna

MANTEGNA'S *Parnassus* (fig. 33) has had the singular misfortune of being praised for the very qualities which it attempts to mock:

> *The God of War and the Goddess of Beauty have seldom been more nobly portrayed than in these triumphant figures, who stand high upon Parnassus, rulers of the sacred mount. Below them, to the music of Apollo, the Muses dance in stately measure — all but one, who has bounded in with swifter movement, thereby indicating perhaps Terpsichore herself. In the foreground stands Mercury, lord of eloquence, leaning on Pegasus — a fantastic beast, mild and beautiful, wings spreading from his sides, his neck hung with great glowing jewels. Behind rises the Pierian hill, source of the sacred stream, which, flowing under the rocks, emerges at our feet.*[1]

Alas, the love of Mars and Venus is a frivolous matter, a subject of uncontrolled mirth for the gods of Homer;[2] for "unquenchable laughter arose among the blessed gods" when they saw the pair exposed by the injured husband, Vulcan. He is present in Mantegna's picture, clamoring

[1] M. Cruttwell, *Mantegna*, 1901, p. 95. The quotation is chosen at random to illustrate a type.

[2] *Odyssey* VIII, 326.

from out his cave (fig. 39), while an insolent cupid pipes at him through a long thin trumpet:

> Cuckoo, Cuckoo: O word of fear
> Unpleasing to a married ear.

Near the entrance to Vulcan's cave is an ominous decoration — a cluster, suitably colored, of sour grapes (ὄμφακες); and the wild rock formation above the cave suggests an arrested volcanic eruption. These mocking traits have not escaped unnoticed; an anonymous French critic understood them precisely:

> *Chose curieuse . . . c'est une des rares toiles où son génie sévère essaye un sourire . . . car ce Vulcain qu'un Amour lutine avec sa sarbacane et qui maudit son épouse infidèle est une "gauloiserie" unique dans l'œuvre du peintre!* [3]

It is fitting therefore that Mars should be represented as a young gallant (fig. 36), and Venus with the humorous expression of φιλομμειδὴς Ἀφροδίτη, "the laughter-loving Venus." [4] The two gods of poetry who celebrate the happy pair — Apollo in the company of the Muses, and Mercury leading Pegasus — are the two brothers who in Homer's council of the gods defended Mars and Venus and amused the gods at the expense of Vulcan: "and laughter arose among the immortal gods." [5]

The spirit of mockery is reflected in the frolicking dance of the Muses; for it is a dancing song which Apollo plays (as in Homer's account, where the love of Mars and Venus and the derision of Vulcan are sung to the lyre as accompaniment for a dance).[6] The four Muses on the right are frivolous damsels whose concern with love is unmistakably expressed by the playful gesture of the concluding pair (fig. 38). The bouncing Muse is the most frivolous of the nine — Polyhymnia who "speaks by gestures":

[3] *Mantegna (Classiques de l'Art)*, Paris 1911, p. xxvi. The frivolity of the *Parnassus* was also observed by Förster, but he inferred that it must be an allegory of vice ("Studien zu Mantegna und den Bildern im Studierzimmer der Isabella Gonzaga," *Jahrbuch der Preussischen Kunstsammlungen*, XXII, 1901, p. 78ff.).

[4] *Odyssey* VIII, 362.

[5] *Ibid.*, 343.

[6] *Ibid.*, 250ff.

Signat cuncta manu loquiturque Polymnia gestu.[7] Erato assists her in this obvious pantomime, the import of which is not lost upon their two neighbors, Terpsichore and Thalia, who react to it with amusement: *Comica lascivo gaudet sermone Thalia.* At the other end of the group, the heroic Muses, Calliope and Clio, make the same gesture toward the back; and a sublimely hypocritical nymph (I presume, the "sweet-voiced" Euterpe) is joined by Melpomene (fig. 37), who is easily recognized by her tragic mask, which is an arresting grimace: *Melpomene tragico proclamat maesta boatu.* The Muse in the center is pictured with averted face — an attitude not uncommonly assigned to Urania (for example, in Raphael's *Parnassus*) so as to characterize her as the "transcendent" Muse, facing the beyond (fig. 35).[8]

While Apollo plays the lyre for this sportive dance,[9] the scene is pre-

[7] *Nomina Musarum* (Loeb Library, Appendix to Ausonius, II, 1921, p. 280). In the Renaissance these epigrams were generally thought to be by Vergil (cf. C. Ripa, *Iconologia*, 1618, *s.v. Muse*). Gyraldus, however, referred to them as "incerti autoris" ("De Musis Syntagma," *Opera Omnia*, I, 1696, p. 565).

[8] The frivolous Muses being placed on the right, the heroic Muses on the left, and the transcendent Muse in the middle, the whole group may be read as a humorous expansion of the classical group of the Three Graces, to which Renaissance Neoplatonists applied the dialectic of Proclus' *Platonic Theology*. See the triadic inscriptions on the medals designed for Giovanna Tornabuoni (fig. 34) and for Pico della Mirandola (G. F. Hill, *A Corpus of Italian Medals*, 1930, no. 998, 1021). Corresponding arguments in Marsilio Ficino (*Commentarium in Convivium Platonis de Amore* I, 4; II, 2; V, 2; also "De Tribus Gratiis et Concordia," *Opera*, 1561, I, p. 890) and Pico della Mirandola (*Conclusiones . . . de modo intelligendi hymnos Orphei*, no. 8; also Girolamo Benivieni, *Canzona dello Amor Celeste e Divino, col Commento d. ill. . . . Giovanni Pico Mirandolano*, bk. II, ch. 2ff.). The subject has recently been encumbered by E. Gombrich ("Botticelli's Mythologies: A Study in the Neoplatonic Symbolism of his Circle," *Journal of the Warburg and Courtauld Institutes*, VIII, as of 1945, published 1947, p. 7–60) who, having "had no difficulty in collecting a round dozen of different exegetic interpretations" of the Three Graces (p. 36), seems unware that the rules for interpreting these triadic images and arguments are to be found in Proclus, *The Elements of Theology* (ed. E. R. Dodds, 1933, Proposition 148, p. 131, also p. 277), the basic textbook of Renaissance Neoplatonism and the model of both Ficino and Pico (*ibid.*, p. XXXII, with further literature).

[9] The lines 1–19 of the mock-heroic poem *Culex* ("The Gnat," cf. Vergil, Loeb Library, II, 1940, p. 370f.) could have served as a model for the group of Apollo and the dancing Muses. Now generally excluded from the Vergilian canon (*ibid.*, p. 368f., 523–527), the *Culex* was a favorite poem of Renaissance hu-

sided over by Mercury, the Arcadian god, who supervises these pastoral rites. He holds a little pastoral pipe and a huge caduceus (the soporific staff by which he lays asleep the volitions of men and awakens their vegetative instincts).[10] Pegasus, the symbol of poetic flight, is under his power, thoroughly tamed and of a lamb-like compliance, charmingly vain with his string of beads, and benevolently grinning (fig. 40).

There was, of course, a classical precedent for representing Mercury as a tamer of Pegasus. He appeared in this role on a medal of Antinous which was copied (if not forged) in the Renaissance (fig. 42) [11] and interpreted as a symbol of *fama chiara* (fig. 43).[12] That this connotation entered into Mantegna's design is suggested by the long trumpet on which Cupid is blowing – the typical trumpet of fame. However, the fact that it is blown by Cupid, and for the purpose of silencing the jealous Vulcan, is proof that *fama chiara* in this case is meant to be *fama d'amore*. The illicit love between Mars and Venus was easily ennobled by allegory. In discussing the love and procreation of the gods as metaphors for universal forces in nature, Leone Ebreo explained in his *Dialoghi d'Amore* [13] that "when this union of the two parents occurs regularly in nature, it is called marriage by the poets, and the partners are called husband and wife; but

---

manists. See Bembo's elegant dialogue "De Culice Vergilii," *Opera*, III, 1567, p. 82–110, in which Pomponio Leto and Ermolao Barbaro are the interlocutors; also the venomous polemic between Politian and Bartolommeo Scala, occasioned by the gender of *culex* (Politianus, "Epistolarum Lib. XII," *Opera Omnia*, 1519, fol. 102v–106v). A charming poem by Celio Calcagnini, *Encomium Culicis*, in *Delitiae CC. Italorum Poetarum*, ed. Ranutius Gherus [i.e. Ianus Gruterus], I, i, 1608, p. 517.

[10] Pico della Mirandola, *Conclusiones . . . in doctrinam Platonis*, nos. 9 and 10.

[11] G. F. Hill, *The Gustave Dreyfus Collection*: *Renaissance Medals*, 1931, no. 405; R. H. Lawrence, *Medals by Giovanni Cavino, the 'Paduan,'* 1883, p. 16, no. 51. The ancient coin is listed as genuine by J. Eckhel, *Doctrina Numorum Veterum*, II, vi, 1828, p. 532, and B. V. Head, *Historia Numorum*, 1911, p. 419; as spurious by G. Blum, "Numismatique d'Antinoos," *Journal International d'Archéologie Numismatique*, XVI, 1914, p. 36, no. 3A. On unquestionable Antinous coins of this type, the horseman holds a caduceus, but the horse is wingless (fig. 41); cf. Blum, *op. cit.*, p. 53, no. 1; p. 58, no. 4.

[12] Ripa, *Iconologia*, *s.v. Fama.*

[13] Ed. S. Caramella, 1929, p. 108; tr. F. Friedeberg-Seeley and J. H. Barnes, 1937, p. 122.

when the union is an extraordinary one, it is styled amorous or adulterous, and the parents who bring forth are called lovers." [14]

It is in praise of such an extraordinary conjunction – the god of battles uniting with the goddess of love, *rerum concordia discors* [15] – that Apollo sings and the Muses dance and Amor blows his fanfare, regardless of the protests of the Philistines (*βάναυσοι*) represented by the *Dunkelmann*, Vulcan. However, in the foreground of the picture there are warning indications that these Arcadian rites are to be attended by purging. Two scourges lie in front of Apollo. And while the presence of the rabbit implies fertility ("for you know, I imagine, what is said of the hare, that it possesses the gift of Aphrodite to an unusual degree" [16]), a more forbidding thought is suggested by the porcupine, a heroic emblem used by Lodovico Gonzaga with the disconcerting inscription *Noli me tangere* (fig. 44, 45).[17] In medieval and Renaissance bestiaries the porcupine was credited with throwing forth its quills when attacking an enemy.[18] This armored animal is a fitting counterpart to Mars, just as the rabbit is an attribute of Venus. Down to these minor details, Mantegna's picture demonstrates the union of contraries – that great commonplace of Renaissance thought which pervades Cusanus' *Docta Ignorantia* as it does Politian's *Panepistemon*, but upon which Shakespeare looked with scorn:

These contraries such unity do hold,
Only to flatter fools and make them bold.

[14] This may explain the otherwise paradoxical fact that some of the same authors who celebrate Harmonia as an offspring of Mars and Venus, insist on the adulterous character of their union. See E. Panofsky, *Studies in Iconology*, 1939, p. 163, n. 120, 121.

[15] Horace, *Epistulae* I, 12, 19; Ovid, *Metamorphoses* I, 433; Lucan, *Pharsalia* I, 98; Lactantius, *Institutiones Divinae* II, 9, 17 (Migne VI, 309, cap. x).

[16] Philostratus, *Imagines* I, 6 (Loeb Library, 1931, p. 27).

[17] Hill, *A Corpus of Italian Medals*, no. 407 (Pietro da Fano).

[18] In an allegory of the League of Cambrai (Pierre Gringore, *Les Abus du Monde*, 1509; cf. *The Animal Kingdom*, The Pierpont Morgan Library, 1940, p. 54f.), the heroic porcupine, which is here to be identified with Louis XII of France, throws its quills at the Venetian lion. A more humble role is assigned to the porcupine on the title page of Sidney's *Arcadia*, where it serves to counterbalance its lowly double – an ordinary swine

In painting the *Parnassus*, Mantegna conformed to the program invented by a Mantuan humanist, presumably Paride da Ceresara. We know for certain that it was Paride who supplied the various "inventions" sent by Isabella to Perugino, Bellini, and Costa; and from her manner in thanking him for his speed and patience in conceiving them, it is evident that he constantly advised her in these matters. Paride was born in 1466, and his friendship with the Gonzagas can be traced as early as 1494 and continued to the time of his death in 1532.[19] He was thus the only humanist in Isabella's circle who is known to have directly witnessed the entire history of her Camerino, from the first painting completed by Mantegna in 1497 to the last picture finished by Correggio about 1530–1532.[20]

---

presuming to sniff at a rosebush which carries the inscription: *Non tibi spiro* (fig. 46).

[19] A. Luzio and R. Renier, "La Coltura e le Relazioni Letterarie di Isabella d'Este Gonzaga," *Giorn. Stor. d. Lett. Ital.*, XXXIV, 1899, p. 86–90. This is the most comprehensive account of Paride da Ceresara, and supersedes G. Tiraboschi, *Storia della Letteratura Italiana* VII, ii, 1824, p. 708f.

[20] Equicola, who became Isabella's *praeceptor* and later her secretary, cannot possibly have advised Mantegna. He began corresponding with Isabella in 1503, and did not settle in Mantua until 1508, two years after Mantegna's death. For the history of this most obsequious gossip and go-between, see D. Santoro, *Della Vita e delle Opere di Mario Equicola*, 1906, rather than the careless account in N. A. Robb, *Neoplatonism of the Italian Renaissance*, 1935, p. 187. Of earlier literature cf. Luzio, *I Precettori d'Isabella d'Este*, 1887; Renier, "Per la Cronologia e la Composizione del 'Libro de Natura de Amore' di Mario Equicola," *Giorn. Stor. d. Lett. Ital.*, XIV, 1889, p. 212–233; D. Santoro, "Appunti su Mario Equicola," *ibid.*, XV, 1890, p. 402–413; V. Cian, "Una Baruffa Letteraria alla Corte di Mantova (1513): L'Equicola e il Tebaldeo," *ibid.*, VIII, 1886, p. 387–398; and the masterly biographical sketch by Luzio-Renier, *ibid.*, XXXIV, 1899, p. 2–21, which tends to confirm the verdict in Niccolò d'Arco's satirical epitaph (*ibid.*, p. 55). Equicola's book on Isabella's motto, *Nec spe nec metu*, has survived in one copy only (Bibliothèque Nationale, Rés. R. 1160, cf. P. Rajna, "Per qui studia l'Equicola," *Giorn. Stor. d. Lett. Ital.*, LXVII, p. 363). It was composed in 1505–1506 as a birthday present to Isabella from Margherita Cantelmo, Equicola's employer at that time. A characteristic letter by Equicola, 22 November 1505, announcing that this book would show "come si discorre per poetica philosophia, et nostra et antiqua theologia, approprиando *nec spe nec metu* ad tucte," was written to Isabella from Blois (published by C. d'Arco, "Notizie di Isabella Estense," *Archivio Storico Italiano*, App. II, 1845, p. 313; corrected by Luzio-Renier, *op. cit.*, p. 4). While the dates of Equicola's Mantuan period exclude him from a part in the decoration of the Camerino, which was practically completed before he arrived, there is evidence that some twenty years later he "invented" programs and inscriptions for the *Palazzo del Tè* (letter from Equicola to Federigo Gonzaga, 17 February 1522, published by Luzio-Renier,

Though the name of Paride da Ceresara is frequently quoted in recent studies of the relations between Isabella d'Este and Mantegna and Perugino, it is assumed that he was an obscure humanist in her employment ("one Paride da Ceresara"[21]). Yet he was so considerable a personage in his time that his tomb carried the simple but proud inscription: *Paris Ceresareorum ille.*[22] The Gonzagas cherished him as "cavalliero et gentilhomo nostro dilectissimo," as he is called in a letter of Federigo's.[23] Bandello, who addressed him as "nobilissimo ed in ogni sorta di lettere dottissimo," introduced him as the narrator of one of his *Novelle*, which was told in the presence of Isabella d'Este.[24] The "new Vergil," Baptista Mantuanus, dedicated his eclogues to Paride da Ceresara,[25] and a classical threnody by Niccolò d'Arco commemorated him as a master of occult philosophy.[26] Cardanus praised his "more than human genius" (*ingenio plus quam humano*).[27] And when Lucas Gauricus published his collection of horoscopes of famous men,[28] he placed Paride da Ceresara next to Erasmus and gave a concise account of his person, his accomplishments,

---

ibid., p. 15f.). In view of Isabella's strained relations with her son Federigo, Equicola tried to by-pass her in his *Chronica di Mantua*, 1521, by declaring that it was better to say nothing of her than too little.

[21] Panofsky, *Studies in Iconology*, p. 153, n. 82.

[22] S. Bettinelli, "Delle Lettere e delle Arti Mantovane," *Opere*, XI, 1800, p. 179. See also Nicolaus Archius (i.e. Niccolò d'Arco), *Numerorum Libri Quattuor*, 1762, p. 123.

[23] Published by Luzio-Renier, *op. cit.*, p. 90.

[24] *Pt.* II, *Nov.* 5. The story of a great envious passion here told by Paride is dedicated to Calandra who developed from it "un libretto in prosa volgare" entitled *Aura*. This is lost except for a summary in Equicola's *Libro de Natura de Amore*, 1525, p. 39f. It may have been less solemn than has been supposed: *Aura* was the name of Isabella's favorite lap dog, a little bitch known from an epigram written on her death by Baptista Mantuanus (Luzio-Renier, *op. cit.*, p. 69) and from commemorative elegies by other poets (*Giorn. Stor. d. Lett. Ital.*, XXIII, 1899, p. 44–47).

[25] *The Eclogues of Baptista Mantuanus*, ed., with introduction and notes, by W. P. Mustard, 1911, p. 62. The first edition, 1498, entitled *Bucolica seu Adolescentia in decem Eglogas divisa.*

[26] Nicolaus Archius, *op. cit.*, p. 79–81. This incidentally answers a question raised by Luzio-Renier (*op. cit.*, XXXIV, p. 90, n. 3) concerning Paride's experience in medicine.

[27] Hieronymus Cardanus, "Liber Duodecim Geniturarum," *Opera*, V, Lyon, 1663, p. 545–549. Cardanus' informant was a pupil of Paride da Ceresara, a Benedictine monk named Evangelista Brasca, created bishop by Paul III.

[28] Lucas Gauricus, *Tractatus Astrologicus*, Venice 1552, p. 65v.

and his "regal palace," adding that "with approaching old age he became preoccupied with astrology." [29] His palace is mentioned also by Vasari, who says that its façade was painted by Pordenone.[30] Popular imagination appears to have been fascinated by this magnificent dwelling, which, from the reputation of its owner as a necromancer, acquired the name of *palazzo del diavolo.*

Obviously, Paride was not one of Isabella's intellectual servants, like Capilupi, Equicola, Calandra, or Bardellone, but a gentleman of substance with whom she exchanged intellectual courtesies.[31] This also explains the tone of her letters to him: "I really do not know who suffers more from the interminable delays of these painters, I . . . or you . . ." This is not the way in which she would address her secretary or *praeceptor* engaged on a scholastic errand. To find a true parallel to Paride's role in her milieu, we must therefore look not to Equicola or Calandra, but rather to her kinsman and favorite poet, Niccolò da Correggio,[32] or to her Bolognese friend, the Magnifico Girolamo Casio, who styled himself "cavaliere et laureato." [33] The members of her household might well be engaged in carrying out her many incidental assignments, but when it came to design-

[29] "Erat facie et barbitio rufus, procerae staturae, sed proportionatus; ex Iove in horoscopo cum Marte ditissimus et locuplex; habebat aedes regias; ingeniosus, legum professor, in litteris latinis et graecis eruditus. Quum senectutis limina fuit ingressus, incepit dare operam astrologiae . . ."

[30] Vasari, "Life of Pordenone." By the end of the eighteenth century the paintings had vanished except for the frieze which was inscribed: *Ceresareorum et amicorum domus.* Cf. S. Bettinelli, *op. cit., Opere,* XI, 1800, p. 179. According to a letter by Federigo Gonzaga, 26 July 1519, the commission had originally been given to Girolamo Romanino, who proved unreliable (Luzio-Renier, *op. cit.,* p. 90).

[31] He was actually a distant relative of the Gonzagas, his wife being a sister of Niccolò d'Arco, on whose genealogy see A. Pranzelores, "Niccolò d'Arco," *Annuario degli Studenti Trentini,* VII, 1901, p. 40 (table).

[32] Luzio-Renier, "Niccolò da Correggio," *Giorn. Stor. d. Lett. Ital.,* 1893, XXI p. 205ff; XXII, p. 65ff. G. Tiraboschi, *Biblioteca Modenese,* II, 1782, p. 103–135. See also A. Baschet, "Recherches de Documents d'Art et d'Histoire dans les Archives de Mantoue," *Gazette des Beaux-Arts,* XX, 1866, p. 485, n.

[33] His *Libro intitulato Cronica, ove si tratta di Epitaphii di Amore et di Virtute (versi tremillia et cinquecento),* 1525, noteworthy as one of the most inept productions of the Renaissance, was dedicated to Ercole Gonzaga, and satirized by Berni. Cf. Antonio Virgili, *Francesco Berni,* 1881, p. 136.

ing the master plan of her Camerino, she applied to a learned Mantuan *gentilhomo*, who had a taste similar to hers for elegantly obscure erudition. This ranged in his case from Greek and Latin to Hebrew,[34] included the law, and wound up in astrology.

Mantegna's archaeological imagination was aroused rather than hampered by this kind of learning, which seemed to supply him with just the right themes for a precise and yet fantastical elaboration. While it is tedious to read the poetical pedants in the circle of Isabella, their fussy "inventions" become persuasively lucid when transposed by Mantegna into a pictorial argument. An aesthetician might be tempted to infer that ideas which make such bad reading should be particularly well suited for good painting, and a musician might confirm this opinion by pointing to operatic *libretti.* But there must be a flaw in this argument since no texts ever aroused the pictorial imagination more strongly than Dante's *Inferno* and Petrarch's *Trionfi.* From all that is known of Mantegna's character, he inclined to be somber, sullen, and violent, a reputation that is borne out by the severity of his pictorial style. It is to the credit of Paride da Ceresara, if it was he who devised the program of the *Parnassus*, that he hit upon the hidden streak of Mantegna's wit and revealed him as a master of the mock-heroic. Paride's own sense of humor is attested by Bandello who, in dedicating a very facetious story to him, described him as "uomo Terenziano."[35]

Mantegna's picture with a grotto for its central motif was the first painting planned and executed for the Grotta of Isabella (1497). A few years later (1502), Mantegna completed its counterpart,[36] *Minerva Ex-*

[34] Cf. Luzio-Renier, *Giorn. Stor. d. Lett. Ital.*, XXXIV, 1899, p. 87.

[35] *Pt.* I, *Nov.* 17. Paride is mentioned three times in the *Novelle* (cf. *Tutte le Opere*, ed. F. Flora, I, 1934, p. 182, 193f, 695).

[36] A letter from Alberto da Bologna to Isabella of 3 July 1497 refers to the hanging of the first picture (G. Fiocco, *Mantegna*, tr. J. Chuzeville, 1938, p. 184). On 25 June 1501, there is still mention of only one picture in a letter from Vianello, but on 22 November 1502 Isabella writes of "the pictures (*li quadri*) of Mantegna" (Kristeller, *Andrea Mantegna*, p. 349).

pelling the Vices from the Grove of Virtue (fig. 48) – a somber picture painted in harsh and livid colors, tempestuous in mood and as forbiddingly moral as its companion is carefree. Like the virtuous Daphne, the spirit of the grove is represented as a ghostly tree which lifts a pair of despairing branches like arms (cf. fig. 47), the trunk encircled by scrolls with declamatory inscriptions written in Latin, Greek, and Hebrew.[37] Three of the cardinal virtues, Fortitude, Justice, and Temperance, watch the battle from the sky while Prudence, the fourth, actively enters the scene in the guise of Minerva. The Vices in the pool are depicted in those monstrous and decrepit forms in which Mantegna excels as a master of the horrible; and the volcanic explosion, which in the *Parnassus* happily congeals in mid-air, is here released in a cataclysm: the mountain top bursts and threatens to crush the sinners.[38]

The severity of Virtue and the frivolity of Pleasure are represented in these two paintings as of equal force; for according to Renaissance eti-

[37] The Latin inscription reads: *Agite pellite sedibus nostris/foeda haec vitiorum monstra/virtutum coelitus ad nos redeuntium/divae comites* (cf. Förster, *Jahrb. d. Preuss. Kunstslg.*, XXII, 1901, p. 161). The fluttering scroll on the right indicates that the *mater virtutum* is imprisoned in the rock. The Greek and Hebrew inscriptions have been disfigured by a restorer, but without serious loss, because it was customary in this humanist affectation to repeat precisely the same idea in all three languages (cf. triple inscriptions in the *Hypnerotomachia*, in Erasmus' *Colloquia*, on Pirckheimer's bookplate, on a printer's mark of Petrus de Nicolinis de Sabio, etc.). That Isabella herself could not read Hebrew is proved by a letter she wrote about *littere sacre* to Paride da Ceresara (Luzio-Renier, *op. cit.*, p. 87). As this is dated 30 September 1498, it may refer to the script prepared for Mantegna's painting; she is anxious to get a sample with less flourishes, but is not sure whether the flourishes are not perhaps part of the letters.

[38] A free rendering of the same theme exists by Lorenzo Leombruno, the Mantuan painter employed in his youth by Isabella (C. Gamba, "Lorenzo Leombruno," *Rassegna d'Arte*, VI, 1906, p. 65–70; 91–96). Later, when Leombruno was forced out of Mantua, supposedly by the advent of Giulio Romano, he painted a *Calumny* (Brera, Milan), in which several motifs again recall Mantegna's painting, in particular the *virtus deserta* and the imprisoned *mater virtutum* (cf. G. Q. Giglioli, "La Calunnia di Apelle," *Rassegna d'Arte*, XX, 1920, p. 173–182). On other Renaissance versions of Lucian's *Calumny*, cf. Förster, "Die Verleumdung des Apelles in der Renaissance," *Jahrb. d. Preuss. Kunstslg.*, VIII, 1887, p. 29–56, 89–113; on the literary problem, R. Altrocchi, "The Calumny of Apelles in the Literature of the Quattrocento," *Publ. of the Mod. Language Assoc. of America*, XXXVI, 1921, p. 454–491.

quette, the well-balanced courtier was to admit them both, combining a valiant sense of duty with an easy grace in his amusements. Under the guidance of the Arcadian Hermes, prudery is to be vanquished by poetic wit, but at the same time, Vice must be expelled by Virtue, staunchly led by Minerva. The two gods, symmetrically placed in the composition of the paintings – the Grove of Virtue must have hung on the left, the Grotto of Pleasure on the right – are symbols of conflicting powers in the soul which are to be harmonized as in music. *Harmonia est discordia concors.*[39] Hence, the painting by Perugino to go between the two Mantegnas represents a combat of virtue and pleasure (fig. 62), in which Minerva battles with Cupid, and Diana with Venus, while the "loves of the gods" are seen in the background[40] – a great tournament of divine passion and divine reason with the outcome held in the balance.[41]

It is little wonder that Bellini found this dialectical setting too harsh and argumentative for his manner of painting,[42] or that it required the skill and tact of Bembo to reconcile him with Isabella's plans. Her faith in bookish learning was so great, and the relish she derived from it so closely akin to

[39] Gafurius (*De Harmonia Musicorum Instrumentorum*, 1518) uses the phrase *discordia concors* interchangeably with the classical form *concordia discors* (frontispiece and fol. 2v). The inversion can be traced back to St. Augustine, *Epist.* XVI, 4; also Licentius, *Carmen ad Augustinum*, 130, who in turn may have derived it from Manilius (*Astronomica* I, 142).

[40] J. Seznec, *La Survivance des Dieux Antiques*, 1940, p. 99, relates the subject to the tradition of the *Psychomachia.*

[41] The picture has been mistakenly called *The Triumph of Chastity*. In the contract it is explicitly named "una batagla [sic] di Castita contro di Lascivia," in which Diana and Venus are to be shown "eguale nella vittoria." The full contract published by Braghirolli, *Giorn. d. Erudiz. Artist.*, II, 1873, p. 163–166, together with a series of fifty-three letters referring to this picture alone. An additional letter, from Perugino to Isabella, is in the collection of Mrs. Raphael Salem, Cambridge, Mass.

[42] Isabella accompanied her instructions by sketches, designed under humanist supervision (Braghirolli, *ibid.*, p. 161). Cf. also her letter to Paride da Ceresara, 10 November 1504: "Per fare schizare questa fabula a vostro modo mandarimo lì a vui uno pictore, aciò ch'el bolognese [i.e. Costa] non possi errare" (Luzio-Renier, *op. cit.*, p. 89). This humanist practice was still prevalent in the early eighteenth century: Shaftesbury in Naples dictated his ideas to a young Irish draftsman, named French, and sent these sketches with his instructions to Gribelin for execution (see "Shaftesbury as a Patron of Art," *Journal of the Warburg Institute*, II, 1938, p. 185–188).

that which she got from her musical entertainments,[43] that she sensed no possible contrariety between the demands of erudition and of fantasy. One of the poetic figures carved on a door in her chambers might be the image of her own genius: a female spirit treading on a skull while carrying books on her head and a horn (*una tromba*) in her hand (fig. 74).[44]

[43] P. Canal, "Della Musica in Mantova: Notizie tratte principalmente dall' Archivio Gonzaga," *Memorie del Reale Istituto Veneto di Scienze, Lettere ed Arti*, XXI, 1879, p. 655–774. See also Luzio-Renier, *op. cit.*, XXXIII, p. 49, for further bibliography, and p. 51 for Isabella's curious musical *impresa*, the "invenzione di tempi e pause." A. Einstein, *The Italian Madrigal* (in preparation), ch. I, discusses composers and musicians in the employment of Isabella.

[44] Presumably Clio, the Muse of history (cf. Ripa, *Iconologia, s.v. Muse: Clio*). The horn, being empty, is not a cornucopia, but of the same type as in Virgil Solis' *Fama* (R. van Marle, *Iconographie de l'Art Profane*, II, 1932, fig. 202). For a full illustration of the door, see G. and A. Pacchioni, *Mantova* (*Italia Artistica*, no. 103), 1930, p. 56. Its precise history and authorship are unknown: the attributions to Tullio Lombardo or Giancristoforo Romano are conjectural. Cf. A. Venturi, "Gian Cristoforo Romano," *Arch. Stor. d. Arte*, I, 1888, p. 50.

"Messer Zuan Bellini's Malady"

PIETRO BEMBO was ideally suited for the role of Isabella's ambassador to Bellini.[1] As a master of elegiac verse (and a perfect exemplar of Venetian manners) he was by temperament predisposed in favor of Bellini's style.[2] At the same time, he was respected by Isabella as an eminent intellect after her own fashion and a courtier of punctilious grace. His gift for being at home in different climates imparted an air of ubiquity to his person as well as to his literary habits. Renowned as the most fastidious of Latin versifiers and a Ciceronian stylist of unmatched perfection, he yet so favored the vernacular speech that he became one of the leaders in bringing Italian back into use as a literary and poetic language.[3] Moreover, he had some pretensions to being a philosopher,

[1] The best contemporary biography of Bembo is by Lodovico Beccadelli (*Monumenti di Varia Letteratura*, I, ii, 1799, p. 223–267). For a critical review of other biographies, including the basic essay by G. Mazzuchelli, *Scrittori d'Italia*, II, ii, 1760, p. 733–769, see the penetrating study by Cian, *Un Decennio della Vita di M. Pietro Bembo*, p. 1–3; for additional literature, his more oratorical summary "Pietro Bembo: Quarantun anno dopo," *Giorn. Stor. d. Lett. Ital.*, LXXXVIII, 1926, p. 225–255. A good bibliography in M. Santoro, *Pietro Bembo*, 1937.

[2] Bembo's sonnet *O imagine mia celeste e pura* (*Rime*, Venice, 1552, p. 7) refers to Bellini in the fifth line. On this poem and the painting to which it alludes, see Vasari, "Lives of the Bellinis"; the same account embellished and expanded in C. Ridolfi, *Le Maraviglie dell'Arte*, I, 1648, p. 56. G. M. Richter, "A Portrait of a Lady by Giovanni Bellini," *The Burlington Magazine*, LXIX, 1936, p. 3f., adds an attractive but hardly tenable conjecture.

[3] *Prose nelle quali si ragiona della Volgar Lingua*, 1525. Aldus, who had launched Bembo as a neoclassic author (*De Aetna*, 1495), recognized him also as the ideal editor of *Le Cose Volgari di Messer Francesco Petrarcha*, 1501. Toffanin's great essay on Bembo in *Il Cinquecento*, 1929, p. 84–103, appeared under the heading *L'umanesimo volgare*, and in his *Storia dell' Umanesimo*, 1933, the same author went so far as to call him "il Lutero del volgare italiano" (p. 289). A less extravagant but equally emphatic statement in G. degli Agostini, *Scrittori Viniziani*, I, 1752, p. xvi.

though not of the scholastic kind. His dialogues on love, *Gli Asolani* (dedicated to Isabella's sister-in-law, Lucrezia Borgia) are distinguished by the fluency of their argument. Written in a rhapsodic prose interspersed with Petrarchan songs, the book is an easy guide through the three Platonic stages of love – Part I, chaotic; Part II, harmonious; Part III, transcendent or divine – which philosophers had discussed in unreadable language. His debt to these pedants is as great as his disdain for them: "I do not want, Lavinello, to reason and argue with you so subtly as one might do among philosophers and in the schools," says the exponent of divine love in the *Asolani*. Hence it is no wonder that in a timid book like the *Cortegiano*, Bembo should be hailed as a Platonic mystagogue.[4]

Realizing that Bellini could never paint, even if he chose to, the kind of crisply dogmatic program invented by Paride da Ceresara, Bembo felt inclined to devise a pagan fantasy which would both suit Bellini's manner and fit into Isabella's Grotta, and so he gave Isabella hope that "the fortress would soon surrender." With pedagogical tact, he explained Bellini's requirements to her: "Sharply defined terms do not lend themselves to his style, being accustomed, as he says, always to roam at his pleasure in painting" (*che molto signati termini non si dian al suo stile, uso come dice di sempre vagare a sua voglia nelle pitture*).[5]

That Bembo and Bellini came to an understanding is proved by Isabella's correspondence.[6] On 6 November 1505, she wrote to Bellini,

[4] On the other hand, it is curious that it should have been Browning (of all English poets) who thought of writing *Asolando*. A refreshing antipathy to Bembo is expressed in the eighteenth century maledictions of Baretti, "La Frusta Letteraria," *Opere*, II, 1838, p. 298–307.

[5] G. Gaye, *Carteggio Inedito d'Artisti dei Secoli XIV, XV, XVI*, II, 1840, p. 76. The translation of this famous letter in Cartwright, *op. cit.*, I, p. 357f., is only a paraphrase, and partly erroneous.

[6] The *résumé* of this correspondence in Cartwright, *ibid.*, p. 354–361, is useful as a guide to the documents, but often inexact in their rendering. For verification, see Gaye, *Carteggio*, II, p. 71–82; C. d'Arco, *Delle Arti e degli Artefici di Mantova*, II, 1857, p. 57–65; V. Cian, *Un Decennio nella Vita di M. Pietro Bembo*, 1885, p. 107f., 218; and particularly "Pietro Bembo e Isabella d'Este Gonzaga," *Giorn. Stor. d. Lett. Ital.*, IX, 1887, p. 103–109, by far the best summary available.

praising and thanking him for having finally consented to accepting an order for a pagan fantasy, of which Bembo was to devise the program: "Since the Magnifico Pietro Bembo . . . has seen the other inventions in our studio (*che ha viste le altre invention che sono nello studio nostro*),[7] he will be able to choose the invention for the one you are to make." In the same sense, she wrote to Bembo himself (2 December 1505): "I hope your Magnificence will not find it too burdensome to devise an invention in your manner, which may satisfy Bellini (*di fare una inventione a modo suo: che satisfatia al Bellino*); for since you have seen the others in our Camerino, you will be able to choose one which is appropriate, and of varied and elegant meaning (*et di vario et ellegante significato*): for you could not do us a greater pleasure." To this Bembo replied (1 January 1506) that he would attempt to reconcile Isabella's and Bellini's wishes: *Tuttavolta si proccaccierà l'uno e l'altro*. A few weeks later a letter from Isabella to Bembo (31 January 1506) shows that Bellini merely waited for measurements. Though the outbreak of the pest in Mantua prevented their immediate despatch, Isabella's eagerness did not abate, for on 11 May she again wrote to Bembo, begging him *di tener ben disposto il Bellino, et di componere la poesia ad sua satisfactione*, which Bembo (13 May) again promised to do.

The fact that no further correspondence on this subject is known has been construed as decisive evidence that the picture was never painted;[8] but no legitimate inference, either positive or negative, can be drawn from the absence of documents. As a matter of fact, the documents are not quite so silent as has been claimed. In a letter written from Venice to Isabella on 9 January 1507, Lorenzo da Pavia excused himself for some delays of his own by referring to those of Bellini: "I seem to have caught

[7] Cian differs from D'Arco and Gaye in reading "studio vostro," but this must be a mistake.

[8] Cf. G. Gronau, *Giovanni Bellini (Klassiker der Kunst)*, 1930, p. xiv, also D'Arco, Cian, etc. Morelli is among the few authors to avoid this conclusion ("The Borghese and Doria-Pamfili Galleries in Rome," *Italian Painters*, I, 1900, p. 259).

Messer Zuan Bellini's malady"; [9] which would seem to imply that new delays on the part of Bellini followed after the correspondence about the measurements. We know that about the same time Isabella took a decisive step which completely altered her policy as a patroness of art. So as no longer to be dependent upon the whims of distant artists, she settled a painter in Mantua who was to complete the decoration of her Camerino under her own eyes. Lorenzo Costa, who received this unenviable appointment, ingratiated himself with Isabella so successfully that he established an artistic monopoly at her court. That he would not tolerate any rivals is proved by Isabella's correspondence with Francia, who delayed about as long as Bellini before beginning a painting Isabella had ordered from him. The two cases are precisely parallel, even the dates coincide; for at the very time when Bembo began negotiating with Bellini (27 August 1505), Girolamo Casio began his attempt to persuade Francia (17 August 1505).[10] Like Bellini, Francia prevaricated; and it is of interest that one of the letters in which Francia tried to resume his contact with Isabella is dated as late as 1511 – six years after the first negotiations: "I hear from Girolamo Casio," so the letter begins, "that Your Highness would like me to paint the canvas for your Camerino which was ordered in past years by our mutual friend." [11] But Isabella was adamant in rejecting Francia's services, even though Lucrezia d'Este, Isabella's half sister in Bologna, tried to intervene in his favor. "And you must also remember," Isabella wrote to her sister, "that, if we received Francia here, we should not know how to do this without offending Costa, and should find it difficult to retain his friendship." [12]

Though it is dangerous to reason by analogy, two inferences may be drawn from this correspondence with regard to Bellini: (1) The fact that

[9] Yriarte, *op. cit.*, *Gazette des Beaux-Arts*, XV, 1896, p. 228; Cartwright, *op. cit.*, I, p. 361.
[10] *Ibid.*, p. 378.
[11] *Ibid.*, p. 379.
[12] *Ibid.*, p. 383.

he did not complete the *Feast of the Gods* until 1514 does not argue against the possibility that this picture is identical with one devised by Bembo as early as 1506. As we know from the histories not only of Francia, but also of Titian and Michelangelo, a delay of some seven years counted for nothing under Renaissance conditions. (2) Since it would appear from the letter of Lorenzo da Pavia that Bellini was delaying in 1507, he may have found himself in the same position as Francia, no longer wanted by Isabella when he was finally ready to serve her. Costa was called to Mantua in November 1506, after the death of Mantegna, and his monopoly was secured in the course of three years. "In 1509 the Marquis gave him 1200 ducats, as well as a house and 250 acres of land . . . and granted him the privilege of a citizen of Mantua in a deed drawn up in the most flattering terms." [13]

These circumstances combined seem to provide the answer to the otherwise rather tantalizing puzzle; namely, why it was that the *Feast of the Gods* went in the end not to Isabella d'Este, but to her brother Alfonso, at whose "insistence" it was completed in 1514; [14] for we are faced with the amusing paradox that Isabella ordered from Bellini a "pagan fantasy" which (for all we know) she never received, and that her brother, Alfonso d'Este, received from Bellini a "pagan fantasy" which (for all we know) he had never ordered.[15] Were it not for the exceptional character of the theme in Bellini's *œuvre*, one might dismiss this quaint fact as a coincidence, and assume that the "pagan fantasy" delivered to Alfonso d'Este had nothing to do with the one ordered by Isabella. There

[13] *Ibid.*, p. 376.

[14] According to an entry in the account books of Alfonso d'Este, 14 November 1514, the work was completed "*instante domino nostro*" (Crowe and Cavalcaselle, *The Life and Times of Titian*, I, 1881, p. 174). To my knowledge, C. Gamba, *Giovanni Bellini* (1937), p. 169, is the only author to have suspected ("è un' ipotesi come un' altra") that the painting completed for Alfonso might have been begun for Isabella.

[15] For the dilemma of the traditional view see P. Hendy and L. Goldscheider, *Giovanni Bellini*, 1945, p. 30: "It is not known how Isabella's brother, Alfonso d'Este of Ferrara, succeeded in getting for his own Camerino in the castle of Ferrara what all her efforts had failed to get."

is a further piece of evidence, however, which eliminates this possibility. The picture which Alfonso d'Este received shows the traces of Bembo's invention. Not only does the choice of the subject point to Bembo as Bellini's adviser when he painted this picture, but some of the mythological characters are portraits, and a portrait of Bembo is among them.

The Sources of The Feast of the Gods

IN 1505, when Bembo began to negotiate on behalf of Isabella, he had concluded a prolonged residence at the court of Alfonso d'Este in Ferrara where his father had served as Venetian vicegerent (*vicedomino*).[1] For Alfonso's wife, the celebrated Lucrezia Borgia,[2] Bembo professed very exalted sentiments, which have perhaps been taken too literally by nineteenth-century realists.[3] All we know is that he entertained, and suitably expressed, the elegant passion expected of a poet, pro-

[1] Cf. G. degli Agostini, *Scrittori Viniziani*, II, 1754, p. 211. The precise dates of Bembo's various residences in Ferrara ("quella dolce patria") are difficult to determine because of his many travels. First visit 1497–1500, second visit 1502–1504 (cf. M. Santoro, *Pietro Bembo*, 1937, p. 15–23). On 26 July 1502, he completed his transcripts from Dante and Petrarch (*Cod. Vat.* 3197) in the villa of Ercole Strozzi (Cian, *Un Decennio della Vita di M. Pietro Bembo*, p. 89).

[2] That the legend of Lucrezia Borgia's profligacy has persisted so long is largely due to the poetic and operatic embellishments of Victor Hugo, Donizetti, Dante Gabriel Rossetti, and John Addington Symonds, the latter clinging to the belief that it is "probable that the darkest tales about her are true," while glibly asserting in the same paragraph that "history has at last done justice to the memory of this woman, whose long yellow hair was so beautiful," etc. (*The Renaissance in Italy: The Age of the Despots*, Ch. VII). For a sober statement of the evidence, see F. Gregorovius, *Lucretia Borgia*, tr. J. L. Garner, 1903, p. 175–181. Fuller documentation in the original edition, *Lucrezia Borgia*, 1874.

[3] B. Morsolin, "Pietro Bembo e Lucrezia Borgia," *Nuova Antologia*, LXXXII, p. 388–422; P. Rajna, "I versi spagnuoli di mano di Pietro Bembo e di Lucrezia Borgia serbati da un codice Ambrosiano," *Homenaje ofrecido a Menéndez Pidal*, II, 1925, p. 299–322. These "Spanish love letters" in the Ambrosiana have unduly agitated the imagination of Lord Byron and later professionals. They consist largely of transcripts from older Spanish poems which Lucrezia copied out for Bembo and which he attempted to imitate. That these literary exercises were used as a vehicle for conveying and returning extravagant sentiments of love was in accordance with Renaissance custom. But even the most fervent of Lucrezia's letters are modest compared with those addressed to Bembo by Vittoria Colonna and transmitted to him through the good offices of the bishop of Nocera.

claiming his veneration in the dedicatory letter of *Gli Asolani* and in some of the classical verses of the *Amores*:

> *Atque ego, qui miseros olim securus amantes*
> *Ridebam et saevi regna superba Dei,*
> *Spectabamque mari laceras de littore puppes,*
> *Nunc agor in caecas naufragus ipse vias.* [4]

The wedding of Alfonso and Lucrezia had taken place in 1502 and was attended by festivities in which the role of Isabella was nothing if not formidable.[5] While she pretended to detest the celebrations, her prominence and display were almost greater than those of the bride, and the ladies of her suite rejoiced at the prospect that "we shall bring the prize home to the house of our mistress." [6] To commemorate the event in mythological disguise by a painting suitable for her Grotta might have pleased the learned taste of Isabella; and this would also have satisfied the diplomatic finesse of Bembo who played the precarious role of a mediator between the two reigning ladies of Ferrara and Mantua. *Causa pudenda quidem, sed tamen apta deo.* The theme seems to have been chosen to celebrate the marriage – a humorous bacchanal of the gods of antiquity, dedicated to the rites of Priapus.

The proper way of honoring Priapus is told in two famous passages from Ovid's *Fasti.* Jocosely warning his reader that it would be "impermissible and also tedious to narrate the feast of the gods" (*nec licet et longum est epulas narrare deorum*), Ovid disregards his own warning by telling the story twice (I, 391–440; VI, 319–348). In comparing the two passages with Bellini's painting (fig. 1), one can see how certain phrases were stressed and others omitted by the adviser who supplied Bellini with

[4] *Carminum Libellus*, 1552, p. 19f.

[5] A detailed contemporary description in Marino Sanuto, *Diarii*, IV, 1880, p. 222–230; see also J. Dennistonn, *Memoirs of The Dukes of Urbino*, I, 1909, p. 473–483; E. G. Gardner, *Dukes and Poets in Ferrara*, 1904, p. 414.

[6] Letter from the Marchesana of Cotrone to Francesco Gonzaga, 1 February 1502 (D'Arco, *op. cit.*, *Arch. Stor. Ital.*, App. II, 1845, p. 223; Gregorovius, *Lucretia Borgia*, p. 253).

pictorial motifs. The picture shows, in accordance with Ovid, that this is "a feast of ivy-berried Bacchus" (I, 393), that it takes place on the slopes of Mount Ida (VI, 327), that the revelers are attended by satyrs and nymphs (VI, 323), that "each has brought his garland" (I, 403), that some of the nymphs appear "with flowing locks uncombed, others with tresses neatly bound" (I, 405–406), that one "through her ripped robe reveals her breast; another bares her shoulder" (I, 408–409). It is also evident that "wine makes drowsy" (I, 421), but it would be difficult to guess what follows:

Priapus, the ornament and protector of gardens (*hortorum decus et tutela*), is generally represented naked, a *rigidus custos ruris*, as Ovid calls him; but exceptions occur, for example in Cartari's *Imagini de i Dei*, where Priapus wears a cloak (fig. 8). Bellini has dressed him as a gardener and adorned his brow with a vine (fig. 6).[7] He is seen bending over a nymph sleeping near a wooden tub (on which Bellini placed his name). The nymph is called Lotis or, in Ovid's later passage, Vesta, the awesome goddess of virgins. The story says that the god "conceived a wanton hope, and tried to approach her furtively," but as he was about to "draw the garment from off her feet" (*a pedibus tracto velamine*), the ass of Silenus most inopportunely began to bray:

Ecce rudens rauco Sileni vector asellus
Intempestivos edidit ore sonos.

The nymph awakened and fled, and all the gods laughed at Priapus. But the ass was killed for its indiscretion, and ever since an ass is sacrificed to Priapus. *Causa pudenda quidem, sed tamen apta deo.* "The cause is shameful, but beseems the god," says Ovid in defending his story.[8]

[7] A stiff, stalky vine with small leafy bluish-green flowers. The plant has not been identified.

[8] Among classical scholars, the passages in Ovid have remained so famous to this day that this may possibly explain the confusing use made of them by L. Hourticq, *La Jeunesse de Titien*, 1919, p. 148, and 256ff. He applied the relevant verses indiscriminately to Titian's so-called *Jupiter and Antiope* in the Louvre (with which they have nothing to do),

Both the ritual and the anecdotal aspects of the legend have been illustrated before and after Bellini. A "Sacrifice to Priapus" is one of the most arresting woodcuts, and advertised as such in the introduction, of the *Hypnerotomachia Poliphili*, a facetious novel of antiquarian sentiment, published by Aldus at Venice in 1499. The ass, covered with a cross of roses, is sacrificed by nymphs before the altar of the god, while vessels filled with milk, wine, and blood are thrown and broken against the statue.[9] Compared with the symbolic precision of this ritual, Bellini's presentation might appear anecdotal. Yet one need only compare it with a literal-minded rendering of the scene, as in a painting by Giolfino in which the braying ass is placed next to the lovers (fig. 7),[10] to see how the story has been lyrically transfigured and is presented under a veil of suspense. Bellini chose to represent the moment just before the ass began to bray. In his picture the gods are drowsily in attendance as Priapus approaches Vesta, but the ass, wide-eyed and with distended nostrils, is about to sneeze; while Silenus, with his hand on its back, restrains the poor animal in vain. An atmosphere of repose mixed with anticipation pervades the scene as the four chief characters (Priapus and Vesta, Silenus and the ass) are about to enact their ludicrous parts.

---

and to Bellini's *Feast of the Gods* (which they fit more precisely than he knew). Apparently he took Ovid's description to be merely the general prototype of a characteristic *scène de mythologie galante*, and did not realize that it was the specific source of Bellini's plot. He regarded the picture as "bien pauvrement imaginé." Mrs. John Shapley called my attention to these pages, and I was puzzled to find that Hourticq, who himself quotes the story of Priapus and Vesta, describes Bellini's figure of Priapus alternatively as "un Pan sournois" and "un Silène balourd."

[9] In Renaissance poetry, the "Sacrifice to Priapus" became a popular facetious topic. A characteristic example by A. I. Crottus, *Hermione*, Mantua, 1545, p. 78, *Ad Priapum*: "Haec liba, hunc bene mentulatum asellum / tibi Murtia victimat, Priape." For a comprehensive collection of such poems, see *Erotopaegnion, sive Priapeia Veterum et Recentiorum*, ed. F. J. M. Noël, Paris, 1798. In F. Saxl's article "Pagan Sacrifice in the Renaissance," *Journal of the Warburg Institute*, II, 1939, p. 361f., the Priapean scenes appear perhaps too solemnly under the heading, "The Sanctification of Love by Sacrifice."

[10] I am indebted to Mr. Hanns Swarzenski for calling my attention to this picture. Several early illustrated editions of the *Fasti*, which were not accessible to me, are listed in G. Duplessis, *Essai Bibliographique sur les différentes éditions des Oeuvres d'Ovide ornées*

The queer humor in Bellini's representation of the gods is therefore not, as has been so often suggested, merely due to a personal idiosyncrasy of the painter, his extreme old age, or his inexperience in treating pagan subjects. It would seem rather that, presented with the half-frivolous, half-ceremonious text of the *Fasti*, the aged Bellini brought to the occasion a wonderful sense of the fitting. He skilfully answered Mantegna's Parnassus by resuming and restating its comic motifs in the rustic setting of an elegy, devoid of heroic trappings (*multi fabula parva ioci*). If the two pictures were to hang opposite to each other, Mantegna's Mercury leading Pegasus would find a counterpart in Silenus bending over his ass. Moreover, Mantegna's ostentatious swashbuckling Mercury would have a disarmingly suave and elegant double in the Mercury painted by Bellini as the "master of ceremonies" in the *Feast of the Gods*.

But beyond these formal correspondences, there is also an echo of the same moral; for the parable of the rabbit and the porcupine applies to Bellini's story as it does to Mantegna's, except that the roles of god and goddess are reversed, and the style of the burlesque is more rural than antique. To represent the union of contraries, Mantegna required a mythological apparatus involving the Nine Muses, Apollo, Mercury, and Vulcan. Bellini, who preferred a setting in which the gods could freely roam (*vagare*), imparted the same lesson in a lighter Arcadian vein. Priapus, the god of fertility, approaches Vesta, the goddess of virgins; but the perfect union of Passion and Chastity is spoiled by the braying of an ass. The moral merges with the ritual. An ass is to be sacrificed to Priapus.

There is evidence in Bembo's writings that he was preoccupied with precisely this theme. His classical elegies, composed in imitation of Vergil, include a *jeu d'esprit* entitled *Priapus*.[11] In this poem, an immacu-

de Planches publiées aux XVe et XVIe Siècles, 1889. They range from 1501 to 1587.

[11] Bembo, *Carminum Libellus*, 1552, p. 12–15: "Ante alias omnes, meus hic quas educat hortus,/Una puellares allicit herba manus" etc.

late simplicity of diction is made to convey a frivolous jest, the comic passages being heightened by the unexceptional purity of the language. Bembo apparently had set his mind to refining the calculated effects of "polished grossness" by which Beccadelli's *Hermaphroditus* had achieved its notoriety; for Bembo, delicate where Beccadelli is pointed, never deviates from the quiet nostalgic mood of the elegy. Even the inevitable pun which marks the conclusion does not come as a shock, as it would in Beccadelli, but appears as a sprightly ironic phrase.

To do justice to this very academic exercise, one should remember that Bembo belonged to the circle of Aldus' Hellenic Academy, which prepared in 1514 (the very year inscribed on the *Feast of the Gods*) the first critical edition of the classical *Priapea*.[12] Bembo had the peculiar advantage of being able to study these reckless poems with an air of filial piety. His father, Bernardo, had advanced a theory about their authorship [13] and (what was perhaps more important) owned a copy of the *Iowa Virgilii* which Aldus considered so far superior to other manuscripts that he decided to base his edition upon it.[14] Aldus announced these plans in his

[12] C. Calì, *Studi su i Priapea e le loro Imitazioni in Latino e in Volgare*, 1893, p. 12. Strictly speaking, there are two collections of ancient *Priapea*, a small group in the *Appendix Vergiliana* and the major collection comprising about eighty epigrams (cf. *Poetae Latini Minores*, ed. F. Vollmer, II, 1923). Renaissance interest extended to both.

[13] In his dialogue *De Culice Vergilii et Terentii Fabulis* (*Opera*, III, 1567, p. 83f.), Bembo reports how his father questioned Vergil's authorship of the *Priapea* and recognized these poems as a composite work produced in the circle of Ovid, possibly with his participation. On the development of similar views in the Renaissance, see Calì, *op. cit.*, p. 41–44; V. Zabughin, *Vergilio nel Rinascimento Italiano*, I, 1921, p. 123, 145; II, 1923, p. 76, 82, 94f., 125f. The traditional attribution to Vergil dates back to Boccaccio (*ibid.*, I, p. 39, 145), if not to Servius, and was still held by Guarino, Poggio, and later humanists (Calì, *op. cit.*, p. 40), while Politian was among the first to propose the attribution to Ovid (*Miscellaneorum Liber*, no. LIX). The debate has continued to this day (cf. R. F. Thomason, *The Priapea and Ovid*, 1931, with useful bibliography).

[14] On the history of this manuscript see P. de Nolhac, *La Bibliothèque de Fulvio Orsini*, 1887, p. 95–98, 239. Fulvio Orsini acquired it in 1579 from Pietro Bembo's son, Torquato. It is now in the Vatican Library (*Vat.* 3252). A full description in O. Ribbeck, *Appendix Vergiliana*, 1868, p. 31ff.

preface to the 1514 edition of Vergil, which he dedicated to Pietro Bembo. According to the statutes of the Aldine Academy, editorial labors were to be combined with convivial amusement, and no subject was more suited for this dual exercise than a study of the *Appendix Vergiliana* and cognate products of a capricious muse. The same enthusiasts who now embarked on a critical edition of the *Priapea*, had endorsed the hybrid taste and extravagant title of the *Hypnerotomachia Poliphili*. Of this mocking phrase the Elizabethan translator (perhaps wisely) retained only the nostalgic note: *The Strife of Love in a Dream*.

Bellini was no stranger to this thoroughly Venetian form of romantic humor, of which some remarkable anticipations are to be found in his father's sketchbooks (fig. 50, 51).[15] If a title were sought for the *Feast of the Gods*, none would be more fitting than that of the Aldine edition: *In Priapum Lusus*.[16] Actually, Bellini's contact with the printing office of Aldus may have been almost as close as his relation to Bembo himself. As yet, his role in the graphic art of Venetian humanism has not been properly assessed, and it is not impossible that traces of his style may yet be discovered in the woodcuts of the *Hypnerotomachia Poliphili*. I know of no closer parallel in painting to the nymphs in the *Hypnerotomachia* than the pair of nymphs in the *Feast of the Gods*. They have much the same broad rounded foreheads and puppet-like features, and they carry out their humorous mission with the same stiff primitive stateliness. Among the names suggested for the "master of the Poliphilus," Mantegna and Raphael have long been discarded, and only Carpaccio seems to linger on, although the most cursory comparison with the perfunctory construction of his figures and perspectives should remove him from any

[15] V. Golubew, *Die Skizzenbücher Jacopo Bellinis*, II, 1908, nos. XXXV and XXXVIII.

[16] It appeared in 1517: *Diversorum Veterum Poetarum in Priapum Lusus*. Calì (*op. cit.*, p. 114f.) lists twenty-two Renaissance editions of the *Priapea* before this date (1473–1515). All, except one, print the *Priapea* with the works of Vergil. The one exception is an edition of Catullus (1500).

possible connection with the woodcuts of the book. The casual formality of many of the scenes in the *Hypnerotomachia*, such as the feast of Eleuterylida, is so much in keeping with Bellini's style that a connection between the "master of the Poliphilus" and the workshop of Bellini may yet prove the most fruitful of the hypotheses proposed.[17]

Be that as it may, the *Hypnerotomachia*, written as a facetiously sentimental novel around the theme of the *Priapea*, is both in form and content a close parallel to the *Feast of the Gods*, far closer in style than Folengo's *Opus Macaronicum*, the burlesque epic (published in 1517) to which Burckhardt compared "das komische Götterfest des Giovanni Bellini." [18] The analogy can be traced down to the minutiae of diction; for the *Hypnerotomachia* is written in that mixed lingo called Pedantesque, which mellows the severity of the Latin phrases by a predominant use of Italian inflexions, whereas the Macaronic style does rather the reverse, rendering the vernacular idiom more pompous by placing it on the stilts of a classical syntax.[19] Though the two procedures belong roughly to the same class of wit, their burlesque effects are opposed to each other, the Macaronic aggrandizing the vulgar, where the Pedantesque quaintly vulgarizes the grand. Hence, Macaronic humor is ponderous, gross, Gargantuan, of the expansive bulk of the Cinquecento. Pedantesque is delicate, ironic, brittle, the last bloom of Quattrocentist nostalgia. To claim that the whimsy of Bellini's *Feast of the Gods* announces as from a distance the sallies of Rabelais would be to overlook the eerie grace of its idiom.[20] In its mixture

[17] L. Pollak, "Der heutige Stand der Poliphilusfrage," *Kunstchronik*, XXIII, 1912, p. 433f.

[18] *Die Cultur der Renaissance in Italien*, 1860, p. 258.

[19] Symonds, *The Renaissance in Italy: Italian Literature*, Ch. XIV: "Burlesque Poetry and Satire." For Macaronic verse before Folengo, see G. Zannoni, *I Precursori di Merlin Cocai*, 1888; for Folengo himself, "De Theophili Folengi Rebus Gestis et Scriptis," *Opus Macaronicum*, I, 1768, p. i–lv; also Luzio, *Studi Folenghiani*, 1899.

[20] "Mit diesem köstlichen Werk, welches ich noch 1853 bei Camuccini in Rom gesehen habe, nimmt die Malerei der Frührenaissance ihren feierlichen Abschied." Burckhardt, *Beiträge zur Kunstgeschichte von Italien*, 1898, p. 395.

of irony and sentiment, the picture echoes the mood of the *Priapea*, that Arcadian mood of frivolous learning which, as Politian had warned his pupils, was sanctioned by the most formal of poets, Vergil:

> *Nec te lampsacium pudeat lusisse ithyphallum,*
> *Blandaque lascivis epigrammata pingere chartis.*[21]

[21] Politian, *Sylvae* I, 84–85.

Mythological Portraits

THOUGH the story of Priapus, Vesta, and the ass of Silenus explains the plot of the *Feast of the Gods*, the picture embellishes the account in Ovid by a number of incidental features for which the poet offers no clue. Why should Mercury, for instance, be given so prominent a place, and endowed with such a clear and unencumbered physiognomy that Jupiter next to him looks like a secondary figure? And who is the goddess with a bowl of fruit before her, from which she has chosen a quince? Her mythological character is difficult to make out; for she does not wear the turreted crown by which Ovid (VI, 321) characterized the lady of the feast as Cybele.[1] And assuming her to be Demeter or Gaea (equivalents of Cybele), in which case the bowl of fruit might be her legitimate attribute, why does she prefer a quince to all the other fruit over which she is mistress? Moreover, why should her companion, of all possible gods, be Neptune, whom one would rather expect to be fond of an Amphitrite? [2] Yet the trident lies at his feet (fig. 3), so that there is no mistaking his identity (even though the trident looks like a pitchfork).[3]

[1] Ovid himself did not think of Cybele when he described the occasion for this gathering as a "feast of ivy-berried Bacchus." The two passages (I, 393 and VI, 321) contradict each other and refer to two different dates in the calendar of the *Fasti*. Bellini was free to choose between them, and it is obvious that he chose the earlier feast. In H. Cairns and J. Walker, *Masterpieces of Painting from the National Gallery*, Washington, 1944, p. 62, a truncated version of the Cybele passage is printed next to the picture. This improvement is in the best manner of Dr. Bowdler.

[2] From the long list of the loves of Neptune, neither Demeter nor Gaea are absent; but as the offsprings of these unions were monstrous (the horse Arion, the giant Antaeus), it would hardly be fitting to remember them in this context.

[3] As a pastoral group, the pair is

Furthermore, Ovid does not say that at the time of this "feast of ivy-berried Bacchus," Bacchus himself was still a child. And yet the idea of introducing an infant Bacchus (fig. 9) must have been well-considered; for a similar child (or perhaps the same?) was painted separately as an infant Bacchus by an artist very close to Bellini, though hardly by Bellini himself (fig. 10).[4] As for Bacchus' foster father Silenus, he ought to be stout, the fattest and roundest of the gods, a mythological Falstaff, yet Bellini gave him a slender figure and a sensitive, ascetic face (fig. 5).

Behind the barrel on the other side of the ass sits an elderly man "whose brows are wreathed with pine." [5] This is Silvanus (fig. 15). His is one of the most remarkable physiognomies in the picture, far more sharply defined than that of Jupiter, whose face is half covered by his cup, or that of the flute-playing Pan in the background.

All these anomalies are to be explained by the actual occasion which the picture was to commemorate.

A quince is a symbol of marriage and occurs as a common attribute in Venetian marriage paintings (fig. 22), in which the fruit is generally held or touched by the bride.[6] It may be inferred, therefore, that this Bacchic feast dedicated to the rite of Priapus commemorates the marriage between the two persons who are here disguised as Neptune and Gaea. Even the gesture of Neptune would then be closer to convention than might be supposed; for it, again, is not without parallel in Venetian marriage paint-

patterned after the type of Vertumnus and Pomona. In the same way, the juxtaposition of Ceres and Apollo recalls the familiar type of Ceres and Bacchus. But while the formal resemblance to these pastoral types may be of interest in explaining the origin and rustic appearance of these groups, it has no bearing on their iconographical meaning.

[4] The picture exists in triplicate: (1) formerly Benson Collection, London (*Catalogue of Italian Pictures collected by Robert and Evelyn Benson*, 1914, p. 149, no. 75), now Duveen Brothers, New York; (2) formerly Hertz Collection, Rome (J. P. Richter, *La Collezione Hertz . . . nel Palazzo Zuccari*, 1928, p. 43, no. 23, pl. XXIX), now Palazzo Venezia, Rome; (3) Gallery, Cassel. Gamba, *Giovanni Bellini*, p. 171, accepts the not uncommon view that (1) is by Bellini himself. As (2) is an inferior copy, it has suffered less from restorers.

[5] "qui pinu tempora nexa geris," *Fasti* I, 412.

[6] Ripa, *Iconologia*, *s.v. matrimonio;* also Panofsky, *Studies in Iconology*, p. 163.

ings of a rustic type (fig. 23). To identify the couple and some of their attendants as portraits may seem an adventurous procedure at best, and would be reckless if it were based on resemblances alone. Fortunately, the figures have symbolic attributes, and these help to confirm their historical characters, particularly when their mythological parts are not predefined by the plot. The leading role of Mercury, for instance, can be explained by the circumstances attending this particular marriage. When the wedding of Alfonso d'Este to Lucrezia Borgia was being arranged, Alfonso's brother, Ippolito d'Este, was in Rome, where he negotiated the contract, presented the marriage gifts, and set the bride on her journey to Ferrara. His features, known from a medal (fig. 18),[7] reappear in Mercury, the messenger of the gods, who presides over this feast as master of ceremonies (fig. 15).

Alfonso himself favored the role of Neptune, for the Ferrarese, with their splendid fleet in the Po, regarded themselves as a major sea power. Even Alfonso's part as *gonfaloniere della chiesa*, as defender of the faith, was glorified by Titian in an allegory of Conversion which included Neptune as ruler of the sea (fig. 27).[8] A relief of Neptune and Minerva also appeared in Alfonso's alabaster chambers;[9] and Alfonso's son, Ercole II, continued to cherish the same device, with the unfortunate effect that a figure of Neptune, painted for his *Sala della Pazienza* in

[7] Hill, *A Corpus of Italian Medals*, no. 1045.

[8] The picture was seen in an unfinished state by Vasari, who said that it was ordered and invented by Alfonso d'Este ("Life of Titian"). After Alfonso's death Titian retouched it for Philip II, changing the Neptune into a Turk, in allusion to the sea battle of Lepanto (cf. R. Wittkower and N. MacLaren, "Titian's Allegory of Religion Succoured by Spain," *Journal of the Warburg Institute*, III, 1939, p. 138–141). The inference (*ibid.*) that none of the Christian attributes were part of the original design is contradicted by one of Alfonso d'Este's coins, which is inscribed with his title of *gonfaloniere della chiesa* and shows a tree trunk with serpents as in the picture (*Corpus Nummorum Italicorum*, X, 1927, p. 446, no. 34, pl. XXX, 23). Moreover, the flag (*gonfalone*) on the top of the lance would seem very fitting for a *gonfaloniere* painting; and the nude female figure corresponds to Ripa's *Conversione* (fig. 28).

[9] L. Planiscig, *Venezianische Bildhauer der Renaissance*, 1921, p. 224, fig. 232, who locates the alabaster chambers in Bellosguardo, contrary to L. Dussler, *Giovanni Bellini*, 1935, p. 138.

Ferrara (fig. 29), has been mistaken for a portrait of Andrea Doria.[10] In later years Titian painted the features of a bloated and brutal Alfonso d'Este (fig. 21), but we know from a medal made by Niccolò Fiorentino in 1492 that he had a sensitive face in his youth (fig. 19).[11] Bellini's Neptune (fig. 20) could be that youth in a fairly advanced, but far from completed, state of dissoluteness. In fact, this image might be regarded as a missing link between the medal and Titian's painting, for the physiognomies of these two, though fully attested as portraits of Alfonso,[12] are more difficult to reconcile with each other than either of them is with

[10] The picture came from Ferrara via Modena to Dresden (no. 132) and was never in Genoa. Though unquestioned by recent scholarship (R. Wittkower, "Transformations of Minerva in Renaissance Imagery," *Journal of the Warburg Institute*, II, 1939, p. 204), the erroneous association with Andrea Doria dates only from the eighteenth century. The picture has the same height (2.11m.), and belongs to the same lot, as two other pictures which also came from Ferrara via Modena to Dresden (no. 127, 142), while a fourth picture (no. 126) is a pendant to no. 127. Two of these paintings have the documented dates of 1541 and 1544 (G. Gruyer, *L'Art Ferrarais à l'Epoque des Princes d'Este*, II, 1897, p. 344; E. G. Gardner, *The Painters of the School of Ferrara*, 1911, p. 162, n.1). This confirms the suspicion that the date inscribed on the present picture, 1512, which is incompatible with its style, may be the restorer's error for 1542. The picture was restored in 1837 by Schirmer, who also "corrected" the design. In the original state, preserved in an eighteenth century engraving (ill. *The Connoisseur*, LXXIV, 1926, p. 163), the female figure held a cross instead of a javelin, but otherwise the design was modeled after the classical group of *Honos et Virtus* (fig. 30), in which *Honos* appeared as "semi-nuda mulieris imago" (Pierio Valeriano, *Hieroglyphica*, 1575, p. 431). With *Honos* holding a cross, and *Virtus* appearing as Neptune, the allegory may refer to the decisive diplomatic event in Ercole's reign, his reconciliation with the Church which began with the concordat of 1539 and culminated in the spring of 1543 with the Pope's visit to Ferrara. Cf. G. Manini Ferranti, *Compendio della Storia Sacra e Politica di Ferrara*, IV, 1808, p. 51–57; A. Frizzi, *Memorie per la Storia di Ferrara*, IV, 1848, p. 335–342. It would follow that the picture cannot have been painted by Francia, who died in 1517, but that the attribution to Garofalo might be retained (H. Posse, *Die Staatliche Gemäldegalerie zu Dresden*, I, 1929, p. 66, as against E. E. Coulson James, "A Lost Francia Picture in the Dresden Gallery," *The Connoisseur*, LXXIV, 1926, p. 157–163). For the evidence that the picture was painted for Ferrara, cf. also Morelli, "The Galleries of Munich and Dresden," *Italian Painters*, II, 1907, p. 122, 140.

[11] Hill, *A Corpus of Italian Medals*, no. 923.

[12] The portrait in the Metropolitan Museum is not unquestioned as a work of Titian's own hand (cf. P. Hendy, *The Isabella Stewart Gardner Museum: Catalogue of the Exhibited Paintings and Drawings*, 1931, p. 367; also H. Tietze, *Tizian: Leben und Werke*, I, 1936, p. 138: "vielleicht nur eine geschickt hergerichtete Wiederholung"), but there can be no doubt about the identity of the sitter.

Bellini's Neptune. Even so, I would not regard the evidence as conclusive, were it not that the identification of Neptune with Alfonso is corroborated by Alfonso's symbolic use of the trident, and that the cumulative evidence of the other portraits in the picture points to the same conclusion.

The determined humor of Neptune's face in the Bellini painting is compatible with what we know of the mixture of adventurousness and perseverance by which Alfonso managed to preserve his ducal estates against the attacks of three different popes and the plots in his own family. A remarkable inscription on a portrait by Dosso, which shows him as a bacchic votary (fig. 69), proves that he was not averse to letting the riotous amusement of bacchic revels reinforce his political gambles. The inscription records that, two months before the sack of Rome, Alfonso d'Este drank a toast to the impending doom of the papacy with the Connétable de Bourbon, who led the assault on the city:

> ALFONSO DUCA TERZO CON IL FIASCO ET IL BICHIERE CONSERVÒ IL DUCATO DI FERRARA E RICUPERÒ QUELLO DI MODENA E REGGIO QUA[N]DO ALLI VI DI MARZO MDXXVII S'ABOCCÒ CON BORBONE NEL FINALE.[13]

One wonders whether Dosso's painting, commemorating one of the most ruthless moods of Alfonso in a bacchic disguise, hung in one room with the Bacchanals of Bellini and Titian. Some fifteen years lie between this portrait and the *Feast of the Gods*; but Bellini's figure of Neptune already gives a sense of the man who "s'abboccò con Borbone nel finale."

The goddess holding the quince, the symbol of matrimony, would then

[13] *Catalogo della Esposizione della Pittura Ferrarese del Rinascimento*, Ferrara, 1933, p. 164, no. 201. On the meeting between Charles de Bourbon and Alfonso d'Este at Finale, see Gregorovius, *Geschichte der Stadt Rom im Mittelalter*, XIV, vi (ed. F. Schillmann, II, 1926, p. 1309). "Abboccamento" has the double meaning of "political agreement" and "drinking bout." The text is a fitting sequel to the inscription on Alfonso's coin celebrating the death of Leo X: *de manu leonis* (Hill, *A Corpus of Italian Medals*, I, p. 36).

be Alfonso's wife (fig. 24). Despite her famous blond hair Lucrezia Borgia did not strike her contemporaries as very beautiful. They seem to have found her features colorless. The Ferrarese ambassador, observing her during the wedding celebrations in Rome, reported home that she had "a sufficient share of good looks," her agreeable manners making her "seem more beautiful than she really is"; and the Marchesana of Cotrone wrote to Francesco Gonzaga: "La sposa non è troppo bella, ma una dolce cera." [14] Her slightly bent nose and strongly receding chin gave her an unpleasant resemblance to her father, which comes out markedly in the profile shown in her medals (fig. 25, 26).[15] Bellini placed her in a three-quarter view which somewhat neutralizes, but by no means veils, these features.

It would follow that the infant Bacchus is young Ercole, the offspring of the marriage. The age of the child (fig. 9) might serve as an indication of the year in which the final painting was actually begun. As Ercole was born in 1508 and looks four or five years old, the picture could have been started in this form early in 1513; and as it was completed for Alfonso in November 1514 (*instante domino nostro*), it would have taken about a year and a half to paint, which is very quick for Bellini.

The political history of Ferrara would also favor the year 1513; for after the desperate struggle against Julius II, this was the first year of peace for Alfonso d'Este. Julius II having died, the accession of Leo X brought about (only for too short a time) a reversal of the papal policy toward Ferrara, and Alfonso d'Este was reinstated as *gonfaloniere della chiesa.* As Gregorovius observed in his study of Lucrezia Borgia, it was primarily in these years of peace beginning in 1513 that "Alfonso devoted himself to the cultivation of the arts." [16] Certainly it was then that his thoughts first turned to the decoration of his Camerino, an enterprise competitive

[14] Cf. Luzio-Renier, *Giorn. Stor. d. Lett. Ital.*, XL, 1902, p. 318, as against Gregorovius, *Lucretia Borgia*, p. 360.

[15] Hill, *A Corpus of Italian Medals*, no. 231, 232j.

[16] Gregorovius, *op. cit.*, p. 339; Gardner, *The Painters of the School of Ferrara*, p. 148.

to Isabella's Grotta. Presumably Bembo thought this a proper moment to promote the scheme he had devised with Bellini and which no longer suited Isabella's convenience.

The presence of Bembo and Bellini themselves at the *Feast of the Gods* adds to the spirit of the occasion, their roles being perhaps the most quaintly chosen of all. A thin Silenus is so contrary to tradition that the character must have been played by a particular actor. Bembo had a very high domed forehead and a thin bent nose which, in the years when he wore no beard, gave him the distinctive and slightly decadent air of an inveterate aesthete. This is shown in a medal by Valerio Belli (fig. 13), which has the charming reverse of an elegiac scene.[17] When the poet became a cardinal, a patriarchal beard gave the same features a more venerable spirituality (fig. 12, 14).[18] That he polished his exterior as diligently

[17] Hill, *Dreyfus Collection: Renaissance Medals*, no. 386. The design of this medal can be dated within a few days. In a letter written on the last of February 1532, Bembo discussed with Belli whether the figure on the reverse should be draped. On 12 March, he expressed some regret that Belli had made the figure hold a branch (Bottari-Ticozzi, *Raccolta di Lettere sulla Pittura, Scultura ed Architettura*, I, 1822, p. 528f.). According to Varchi, the reclining figure was intended as a river god (*ibid.*, V, p. 199). Of the beardless Bembo, as shown in this medal, no painted portrait seems to have survived, unless the ingenious hypothesis be accepted that Bembo is represented in a much debated portrait at Hampton Court (no. 117), which was left unattributed by Crowe and Cavalcaselle because of its ruinous condition but has been claimed by Berenson and Gronau as a typical late Bellini. See Hendy and Goldscheider, *Giovanni Bellini*, p. 27, pl. 106; B. Berenson, *Italian Pictures of the Renaissance*, 1932, p. 70; Crowe and Cavalcaselle, *A History of Painting in North Italy*, I, 1912, p. 180; Gronau, "Über Bildnisse von Giovanni Bellini," *Jahrb. d. Preuss. Kunstsl.*, XLIII, 1922, p. 104f., also *Spätwerke des Giovanni Bellini*, 1928, p. 20.

[18] The mosaic by Francesco and Valerio Zuccato (fig. 14), dated 1541 and mentioned in Vasari's "Life of Titian," was first published by G. Coggiola, "Per l'Iconografia di Pietro Bembo," *Atti del Reale Istituto Veneto di Scienze, Lettere ed Arti*, LXXIV, ii, 1914, p. 473-514, plate I, 2. Coggiola discusses also the so-called Nardi portrait of Bembo, apparently lost since the late 1870's (*ibid.*, p. 490), but fully described by Crowe and Cavalcaselle who had seen it "in the studio of Signor Vason at Venice" (*The Life and Times of Titian*, p. 418f.). It is copied, I believe, in the engraving by Benaglia (fig. 12), which served as a frontispiece to Bembo's *Opere*, 1808. This engraving shows precisely the "profile" described by Crowe and Cavalcaselle: "A half-length with a characteristic head shorn of hair, but long of beard. A high forehead, gaunt cheeks, and an aquiline nose" (*ibid.*, p. 419). On the somewhat intricate question of the precise periods in which Bembo wore, or abstained from wearing, a beard, and

as his verses may be inferred from his discriminating use of perfumes, among which he gave preference to those manufactured by Isabella d'Este.[19] An unexpected gift for self-derision is revealed in this paragon of refinement by his choosing for himself the role of Silenus (for which he may have been quite suited in one respect only, as tutor of the little Bacchus); and yet he plays the part with such ease that this Silenus looks like a rustic Scapin, and would be quite at home in the *Commedia dell'Arte.*

As for Silvanus, it is not impossible that this is the aged Bellini himself.[20] If comparison is made with the drawing in Chantilly and the woodcut published by Vasari (fig. 15–17), a marked similarity will be found in the shape and angle of the long pointed nose, the pinched mouth, the narrow cheek, and above all in the wistful expression of mellowed shrewdness. The place he has assigned to himself next to the ass and the barrel of wine, and near to (but lower than) Bembo, is of singular humor and modesty. Attending the scene in a corner, the inventor and the executant of the picture present themselves as habitual roamers of those woods in which the gods are assembled for a feast.

How many (if any) of the other figures are portraits is difficult to determine and may be left undecided. The Pan playing the flute is certainly as impersonal a mythological figure as the satyr seen from the back. The presence of such unmistakably neutral characters proves that Bellini mixed his portraits in among general types, and possibly that he introduced transitional figures. No doubt Jupiter, Apollo, and Priapus

---

the chronology of the styles he fancied, see the literature quoted by Coggiola. It would be a mistake to assume with W. Suida, "New Light on Titian's Portraits," *The Burlington Magazine*, LXVIII, 1936, p. 281f., that Belli's medal (fig. 13) shows Bembo young because he is beardless. Hill dates this medal in 1532, when Bembo was sixty-two years old, and this date is supported by the two letters from Bembo to Belli quoted in the preceding note. That Bembo began growing a beard four years later (1536) is proved by a letter from Cellini to Varchi (Bottari, *op. cit.*, I, p. 14–16).

[19] Luzio-Renier, *Mantova e Urbino: Isabella d'Este ed Elisabetta Gonzaga*, 1893, p. 160; also "Il Lusso di Isabella d'Este," *Nuova Antologia*, LXV, 1896, p. 679.

[20] I am indebted to Mr. John Walker for this suggestion.

himself have features as pronounced as Neptune or Mercury, but their features are disfigured by foreshortenings or overlappings. Ceres looks more dishevelled and distorted than Gaea. In contradistinction to these, the six figures discussed as portraits, i.e., Mercury, Neptune, Gaea, Silvanus, Silenus, and Bacchus, retain their physiognomies unimpaired, however burlesque some of their gestures may be. Admitting different degrees of buffoonery, we may suspect that the more grotesque looking deities have perhaps the features of certain court fools, actors, musicians, or other *familiari;* and the same would apply to some of the nymphs.

For princes to meet on an equal level with *litterati* and buffoons and join in their pranks was part of Renaissance etiquette, a custom cherished all over Italy, but cultivated with singular flair at Ferrara, which produced in Boiardo and Ariosto the masters of the mock-heroic style.[21] Bellini's art of lyrical suspense is magically suited for travesty and disguise. His pair of star-crossed lovers near the wooden tub are the closest kin to Titania and Bottom; and perhaps the fairest phrase circumscribing their state is the comment which refers in *A Midsummer Night's Dream* to the mythological play of the clowns: "The best in this kind are but shadows."

[21] G. Bertoni, "Buffoni alla Corte di Ferrara," *Rivista d'Italia*, I, 1903, p. 497-505.

Comus, God of Revelry

IT is not surprising that a painting conceived in the playful style of the *Feast of the Gods* should have appealed to the taste of Alfonso d'Este.[1] Like many other Renaissance princes – for example, the Earl of Southampton, for whom Shakespeare wrote *Venus and Adonis* and the *Rape of Lucrece* – Alfonso had a predilection for mythological *erotica*; and in this he was followed by his nephew, Federigo Gonzaga, Isabella d'Este's son, who, having shared the companionship and tastes of Pietro Aretino,[2] ordered from Correggio the famous *Io*, *Leda*, and *Danae* (not to speak of the *Olympias* and *Pasiphae* painted for him by Giulio Romano). A certain levity of gesture and costume in Bellini's *Feast of the Gods* is probably to be accounted for as an amused concession to the particular tastes of Alfonso d'Este, to which even Michelangelo conformed when he designed a *Leda* for him. But while it may be assumed that in Isabella's Grotta the gods would have acted with a little more decorum, there is no reason to suspect that the theme as such would have displeased her.[3] From her amused remarks on some of the improprieties in the comedies performed at Ferrara, it may be inferred that she

[1] The *Fasti* remained a favorite book in Ferrara. The first Italian translation, by Vincenzo Cartari (*I Fasti di Ovidio Tratti alla Lingua Volgare*, 1551), was dedicated to Don Alfonso d'Este, grandson of Alfonso I. Cartari also wrote the first comprehensive commentary, *Il Flavio intorno ai Fasti Volgari*, 1553. For his literary character, as compared with Gyraldus and Natale Conti, see Seznec, *La Survivance des Dieux Antiques*, p. 199–222.

[2] A. Baschet, "Documents Inédits tirés des Archives de Mantoue: Documents concernant la personne de messer Pietro Aretino," *Arch. Stor. Ital.*, III, ii, 1866, p. 105–130.

[3] Isabella's library included a copy of the *Fasti* (no. 98 in the inventory published by Luzio-Renier, *Giorn. Stor. d. Lett. Ital.*, XLII, 1903, p. 80).

granted levity its legitimate place.[4] In fact, her relish for certain *cose galanti* and her wish to see them represented in her studio were sufficiently well known to induce Salai to offer to paint them for her; [5] and even Perugino tried to make up for the failure of his *Combattimento d'Amore* by presuming that she might accept from him for her Grotta a painting of Mars and Venus surprised by Vulcan.[6]

That the *Feast of the Gods* would have been a suitable ornament for Isabella's Camerino is proved by the important role she assigned in her scheme of decoration to a picture of Comus, the god of revelry (fig. 59). This was made the largest picture of all.[7] Begun by Mantegna and completed by Costa, it was designed as a sequel to Mantegna's Grove of Virtue, in accordance with Cicero's phrase *virtute duce, comite fortuna,*[8] in which the word *comes* was interpreted (in the true spirit of Renaissance punning) as an allusion to the god Comus.[9] In the painting, this word (COMES) is inscribed four times on the gate of revelry,[10] from which

[4] A. d'Ancona, *Origini del Teatro Italiano*, II, 1891, p. 379.

[5] Cartwright, *op. cit.*, I, p. 336.

[6] *Ibid.*, p. 339.

[7] Fig. A (p. 53) shows a reconstruction of the original arrangement of the Grotta, as suggested by the sequence of the acquisitions. Of the Grotta in its final phase there is a complete inventory of 1542 (Document XCI in D'Arco, *Arch. Stor. Ital.*, App. II, 1845, p. 324ff; cf. Luzio, *La Galleria dei Gonzaga*, 1913, p. 205), which records the arrangement as shown in fig. B. The change from A to B was determined by the two Correggios, acquired by Isabella as late as 1530–32. In both plans, the paintings were to be seen in pairs of opposites (along each wall as well as across the room), the only exception being the Perugino, which faced the door to a second chamber containing primarily sculptures. I have disregarded Yriarte's reconstruction (*Gazette des Beaux-Arts*, XIV, 1895, p. 128; *The Art Journal*, 1898, p. 102): it takes no account of the argument of the pictures or of the sequence given in the inventory, and moreover locates the Grotta in a wrong place.

[8] *Epistulae ad Familiares* X, iii (*Ad Plancum*), first printed 1467, traceable in fifty-nine editions before 1500 (*Catalogue of Books Printed in the XVth Century now in the British Museum*, VII, 1935, p. xi; V. Scholderer, *Vom Italienischen Frühdruck*, 1932, p. 11). The device was popularized by Erasmus' *Adagia* (*Cent.* X, 47) and Alciati's *Emblemata* (ed. 1542, no. XVIII), and adopted by Alciati for his own motto (cf. *Grimaldi's Funeral Oration for Andrea Alciati*, ed. Henry Green, 1871, p. VIII), also by Giuliano II de' Medici, etc. (R. Wittkower, "Chance, Time and Virtue," *Journal of the Warburg Institute*, I, 1938, p. 317).

[9] According to Gyraldus, Comus was "deus conviviorum et comessationum" ("Syntagma I," *s.v. Comus; Opera Omnia*, 1696, I, p. 46).

[10] Cf. Kristeller, *Mantegna*, p. 359.

the evil spirits are dispelled by Mercury and Janus. The dedication of the gate thus explicitly matches the inscription on the tree in the Grove of Virtue, which also invoked the *virtutum comites.*[11]

A "gate of revelry" was associated with Comus (fig. 58, 60) because Philostratus described him as "stationed at the doors," which he called a grand "propylaeum" (προπύλαια):

> *. . . golden doors, I think they are; but to make them out is a slow matter, for the time is supposed to be at night. Yet night is not represented as a person, but rather it is suggested by what is going on . . .*[12]

In Costa's painting, too, the gate is meant as a monumental entrance door to the garden rather than a "triumphal arch" (as it has been called), which also explains the presence of Janus. The heroic statues on the gate and the broken column in front of it are symbols of *virtus* and combine with the *comes*-inscription of the gate itself to convey the idea of *comes virtutis.* According to Philostratus, Comus is supposed to be drunk and half asleep, holding a torch downward while he stands next to the gate which opens upon a feast of Hymen. None of the characters in the picture agrees with this description precisely, but the mood of Comus is most fittingly expressed by the drowsy figure in the foreground near the gate, while the god presiding over the feast fully awake and holding a torch (upright) might be Hymen. He is placed between "two Venuses, one draped, the other nude,"[13] and their two cupids. A forward musician trying to

[11] See above p. 18, n. 37.

[12] Philostratus, *Imagines* I, 2. Cf. Förster, "Philostrats Gemälde in der Renaissance," *Jahrb. d. Preuss. Kunstslg.* XXV, 1904, p. 17. The Aldine edition of 1503 combines the *Imagines* with the works of Lucian.

[13] Cf. a letter of 15 July 1506 addressed to Isabella d'Este by Calandra after he had seen the incomplete painting in Mantegna's studio (D'Arco, *Delle Arti e degli Artefici in Mantova*, II, 1857, p. 65f.). For the general tradition of the *Geminae Veneres*, see Panofsky, *Studies in Iconology*, p. 152f. In note 82, Panofsky infers (1) that Bembo was asked to suggest the theme of Comus to Bellini "before Mantegna accepted the commission," and (2) that "Calandra carried on the negotiations with Mantegna." But these observations are not borne out by the correspondence. When Isabella asked

"transcend" the draped Venus so as to approach her sister, is being restrained by the former with a modest and warning gesture. From all of this it is to be inferred that the pleasures in this garden, however sensuous, are pure, a kind of *honesta voluptas* for which Comus-Comes serves as a guardian spirit, a symbol of the reconciliation of Plato with Epicurus.

Bellini was familiar with the belief that revelry should be acceptable as a reward of virtue. He himself had painted an allegory of Comus (fig. 56), a *comes virtutis* graciously offering the reward of pleasure, a Bacchus-like figure (for Comus was the son of Bacchus), comfortably riding on a chariot drawn by cupids and following on the heels of persevering Virtue: *virtute duce, comite fortuna.* As Comus is here to represent good fortune, he bears the attributes of *Bonus Eventus* (fig. 57).[14]

Bembo to find a theme for Bellini, she left the choice to him; there was no suggestion that it should be Comus. And Calandra's negotiations with Mantegna did not concern primarily the picture of Comus, but the sale of a Roman bust. On this occasion he got a glimpse of the picture in progress, of which he sent a description to Isabella; but this letter does not suggest that he had negotiated the commission or played any part in the invention of the design. Nor is it quite correct to refer in this context to Equicola's role as "Isabella's private secretary"; for he was not appointed to this post until thirteen years later (1519). In 1506, he was still in the employment of Margherita Cantelmo. See also above p. 15.

[14] Bellini's allegory served, together with three others of equal size and a fifth slightly smaller panel, as decoration of a mirror (fig. 52–56). Cf. G. Ludwig, "Venezianischer Hausrat," *Italienische Forschungen*, 1906, I, p. 187ff. His reconstruction is, however, untenable: (1) it postulates a sixth panel, of which there is no trace, (2) it does not adequately account for the smaller size of one of the five panels, (3) it is based on an iconographical theory which is contradicted by the visual evidence. The blindfolded harpy with flying forelock (fig. 49) cannot possibly be *Summa Virtus*, even though she is winged and carries the two jugs of Temperance. Nor is *Prudentia* ever represented with so repulsive a face or with an ugly mask in her mirror or attended by little drummers and trumpeters (fig. 53). While the woman in the boat has certainly the attributes of *Fortuna*, she does not look "inconstant." Her maternal affection for the little children might qualify her for a *Caritas*; in fact, the group is led by a jubilant Amor (fig. 54). From the symmetrical use of symbols in the four major panels, I would infer that the mirror was intended for a couple: As *Comes Virtutis* (fig. 56) is the good fortune of man, so *Fortuna Amoris* or *Caritatis* is the good fortune of woman (cf. the juxtaposition of *Bonus Eventus* and *Bona Fortuna*, male and female allegories of good fortune, in Pliny, *Naturalis Historia XXXVI*, 23). These two images of well-deserved fortune are counterbalanced by two warning pictures of evil fame: *Vana Gloria* as the ill fame of woman (fig. 53), and

The entire program of Isabella's Grotta was but an expansion of this poetical theme; and the *Feast of the Gods*, treating of a subject both learned and gallant, illustrated the joys of relaxation which Isabella (no less than Alfonso) was willing to admit in the name of Comus.

Meanwhile, Isabella's studio passed under the direction of Costa, who completed Mantegna's *Comus* in a form which made it a suitable parallel to the picture he himself had painted for Isabella when he was still in Bologna. Generally called *The Parnassus of Isabella d'Este*,[15] this is by far the most stilted composition of the series (fig. 61). As against the innocent pleasures of revelry, it glorifies the more studied refinements of poetry and music. Protected by a valiant knight and an intransigent nymph (*virginis os habitumque gerens et virginis arma*),[16] the garden of harmony opens between two bucolic maidens holding a cow and a lamb respectively, the cow suggesting the husbandry of Vergil's *Georgics*, the

Servitudo Acediae as the ill fame of man (fig. 55). The symbolism of the snail corresponds to Pierio Valeriano, *Hieroglyphica*, 1575, p. 203 (bk. XXVIII, *s.v. cochlea*). The moral that the mirror can be used for good and for ill is summarized in the blindfolded figure of *Nemesis* (fig. 49), which is placed with deliberate paradox above the glass (fig. 52). On her role as winged goddess of chance, retribution, and temperance cf. Gyraldus, "Syntagma XVI," *Opera Omnia*, I, 1696, p. 465, and Alciati, *Emblemata*, 1531, fol. A7r, where both picture and text supply striking parallels to Bellini's image. For the combination of Nemesis with a mirror, see Alciati, *Emblemata*, 1542, no. LXXIX: "Illicitum non sperandum," also an engraving by the "Master of 1515" (Van Marle, *Iconographie de l'Art Profane*, II, fig. 216), where Nemesis herself holds a mirror. Iconographically, the picture of Nemesis belongs so unquestionably to Bellini's mirror and is so brilliant and original in its treatment of the theme that it seems difficult to accept R. Longhi's recent verdict: "nulla ha veramente in comune con la poetica del grande maestro" ("Viatico per la Mostra Veneziana dei Cinque Secoli," *La Rassegna d'Italia*, I, i, 1946, p. 70).

[15] A more correct name is probably *The Garden of Harmony*, in its turn a counterpart to the *Garden of Revelry* (Comus). Cadmus, the dragon slayer and husband of Harmonia, might be the heroic figure on the left. As Harmonia herself was the daughter of Mars and Venus (Hesiod, *Theogony*, 937, 975; Boccaccio, *Genealogia Deorum* II, lxiii; IX, xxxvii), the theme would be a fitting sequel to Mantegna's *Parnassus*. But this is purely conjectural. The suggestion that the man in the foreground is Castiglione (proposed by Gruyer and accepted by Yriarte) must be erroneous. Castiglione had left Mantua in disgrace in the summer of 1504, and was forbidden to enter Mantuan territory in 1505 and 1506. Cf. Cartwright, *op. cit.*, I, p. 270. The program of the picture, again devised by Paride da Ceresara, was sent to Bologna on 27 November 1504 (*ibid.*, p. 373).

[16] *Aeneid* I, 315.

lamb the pastoral poetry of the *Eclogues*, or possibly Boeotia and Arcadia. In the enclosure, a circle of musicians and poets surround a lady (supposedly Isabella d'Este herself) who kneels before a very chaste looking goddess of love and is crowned by a modest Amor, while a heroic bustle on the distant shore intensifies the sense of peace in this idyllic community. Neither the hero nor the nymph in the foreground has been identified; yet it is safe to suspect that the battle scene refers to the hero, the problematic love scene in the right background to the nymph. Though the picture is arranged slightly off center, it is pervaded by a most literal-minded symmetry.

Unfortunately, this insignificant work commemorates the type of poetry which Isabella admired most, the heroic pastoral in which her friend and kinsman Niccolò da Correggio excelled, whose pastoral plays, *La Fabula di Cefalo* and *La Fabula di Calisto* were produced in Ferrara and Mantua.[17] "But the masterpiece in this style," according to Burckhardt,[18] "was the 'Sarca' of Pietro Bembo, which tells how the river-god of that name wooed the nymph Garda; of the brilliant marriage feast in a cave of Monte Baldo; of the prophecies of Manto, daughter of Tiresias; of the birth of the child Mincius; of the founding of Mantua, and of the future glory of Vergil, son of Mincius and of Maia, nymph of Andes. This humanistic rococo is set forth by Bembo in verses of great beauty concluding with an address to Vergil, which any poet might envy him. Such works are often slighted as mere declamation. This is a matter of taste on which we are all free to form our own opinion." [19]

Whether the ceremony in the garden of Costa's *Parnassus* really centers in Isabella's own person, as is generally supposed,[20] is not quite easy to de-

[17] The former is printed in *Opere dell' Illustre . . . Signor Niccolò da Correggio intitolate La Psiche e l'Aurora*, 1515. For the latter, see D'Ancona, *Origini del Teatro Italiano*, II, p. 380; also above p. 16, n. 32.

[18] *The Civilization of the Renaissance in Italy*, tr. S. G. C. Middlemore, The Phaidon Press, n.d., Pt. III, p. 132.

[19] The *Sarca* was published by A. Mai, *Spicilegium Romanum*, VIII, 1842, p. 489–504.

[20] First suggested, I believe, by A. v. Reumont, "Il Quadro Dipinto da Pietro

termine; for though a good deal has been written about her portraits, she herself saw to it that her official countenance remained rather undefined. Her most admired portrait was that by Francia, a gift from her sister in Bologna; but as she would not permit Francia to come to Mantua for fear of offending Costa's sensibilities, this portrait had to be made after a drawing of a much earlier date and seems to have resembled her only remotely. From this painting, now lost, Titian made a copy, which was in its turn copied by Rubens.[21] The semi-archaic charm of Titian's painting (fig. 73), its wooden posture and faintly doll-like head, may be due to the fact that it is a portrait twice removed from the sitter. Yet this seems to have been the form in which Isabella preferred to be remembered; for when Giancristoforo Romano's medal of her was chased for a specimen de luxe, the characteristic matronly features of the primary state (fig. 71) were transformed into a more abstract and delicate profile (fig. 72),[22] not unlike the impersonal literary portrait of her in Trissino's eulogistic *Ritratti*.[23]

Perugino per Isabella d'Este Gonzaga," *Giorn. d'Erudiz. Artist.*, III, 1874, p. 178, and accepted by Burckhardt, *Beiträge zur Kunstgeschichte von Italien*, p. 387.

[21] Luzio, "I Ritratti d'Isabella d'Este," *Emporium*, XI, 1900, p. 344–359; 427–442: a basic study of the documentary evidence.

[22] Hill, *A Corpus of Italian Medals*, no. 221. Hill insists, against Luzio and with G. Habich (*Die Medaillen der Italienischen Renaissance*, 1923, p. 91), that these are two states of one medal, not two different medals. Luzio's own archival researches (*loc. cit.*) leave no doubt that this medal and a conventional marriage coin, which gives only a vague idea of her features, are the only authentic contemporary portraits of Isabella to survive. The cartoon in the Louvre is not by Leonardo, and the identification of the sitter with Isabella rests on the implausible arguments of Yriarte, "Les Relations d'Isabelle d'Este avec Léonard de Vinci," *Gazette des Beaux-Arts*, XXXVII, 1888, p. 118–131. Luzio's own *plaidoyer* for a pseudo-Leonardesque drawing in the Uffizi is admittedly quite a wild conjecture. Unfortunately, several more such conjectures were added by Luzio, *La Galleria dei Gonzaga*, p. 183–238, and Gronau, "Frauenbildnisse des Mantuaner Hofes von Lorenzo Costa," *Pantheon*, I, 1928, p. 235–241.

[23] G. G. Trissino, *La Sophonisba, Li Ritratti*, etc., 1549, fol. 39v–49r. This dialogue was recorded for Margherita Cantelmo and was supposed to have taken place in Milan between Pietro Bembo and Vincenzo Macro after a visit to Demetrius Chalcondylas. Isabella's portrait is here designed, like Zeuxis' picture of Helen, as a composite of the best features of several other women, all of them named. Cf. Cicero, *De Inventione* II, i.

Under these circumstances, the identification of Isabella in Costa's painting is far more precarious than that of the various characters in Bellini's *Feast of the Gods*, particularly as it cannot be supported by the correlative evidence of other portraits in the same picture. Even so, the suggestion might be defended; for it would be quite characteristic of the courts of Ferrara and Mantua, that Alfonso should prefer to be portrayed in a setting of revelry, Isabella in one of pastoral refinement.

Some twenty years later, when Correggio painted his two allegories of *Virtue* and *Pleasure* for Isabella's Grotta (fig. 63, 64), the picture of Pleasure was made to convey the notion of demoniac possession, thus moving away from Philostratus' towards Milton's idea of Comus. The garden-like landscapes in which Correggio placed his figures – a cleanly trimmed bosk for Virtue, but rampant verdure for Pleasure – conform to the setting of Mantegna's pictures, to which they were joined on either side; but the redundant allegorical epithets (anticipating Rubens' Medici cycle) carry the imprint of Stoic oratory. One must imagine Correggio's two pictures at the head of the chamber (fig. B), flanking the entrance door and thereby serving as frontispieces, and one will find that the lightheartedness of Mantegna's *Parnassus* is offset by its being placed directly next to this derogatory allegory of Pleasure, while on the opposite side the apotheosis of Virtue reinforces the ethics of Mantegna's *Minerva*. This shift in moral emphasis is consonant with the novel use of metaphor, in which the attractions of myth are abandoned for the involutions of pure iconology.[24]

Added as a kind of posthumous moral apology to a completed mythological program, these pictures read like those anti-pagan reflections which Gyraldus introduced into his mythological treatises in an attempt to protect them against the bigoted censure which prevailed after the sack

[24] Even the four cardinal virtues no longer appear as separate persons, but are signified by four attributes (the serpent, the lion's skin, the bridle, and the sword), all of them imposed on one single figure on the left who represents "moral virtue," as distinguished from "intellectual virtue" on the right. Cf. above, p. 46, n. 7.

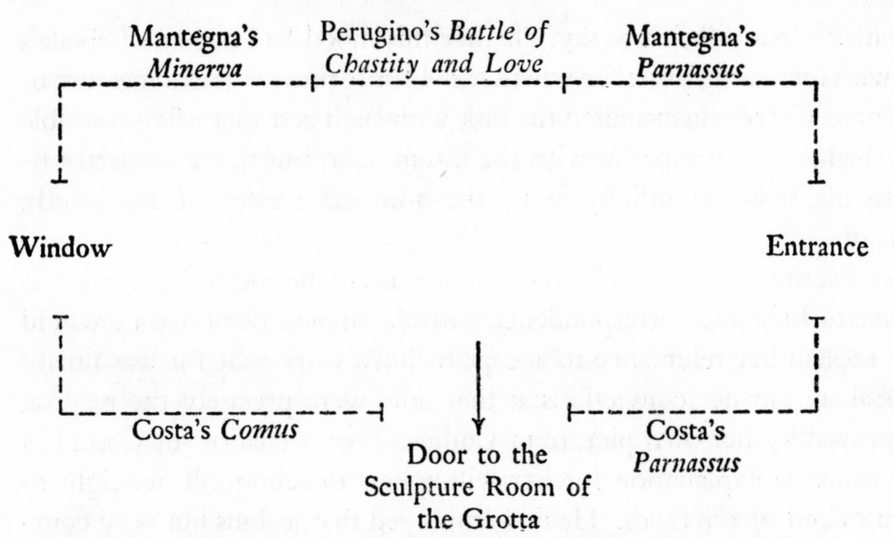

fig. A. CONJECTURED ARRANGEMENT OF ISABELLA'S GROTTA BEFORE 1530.

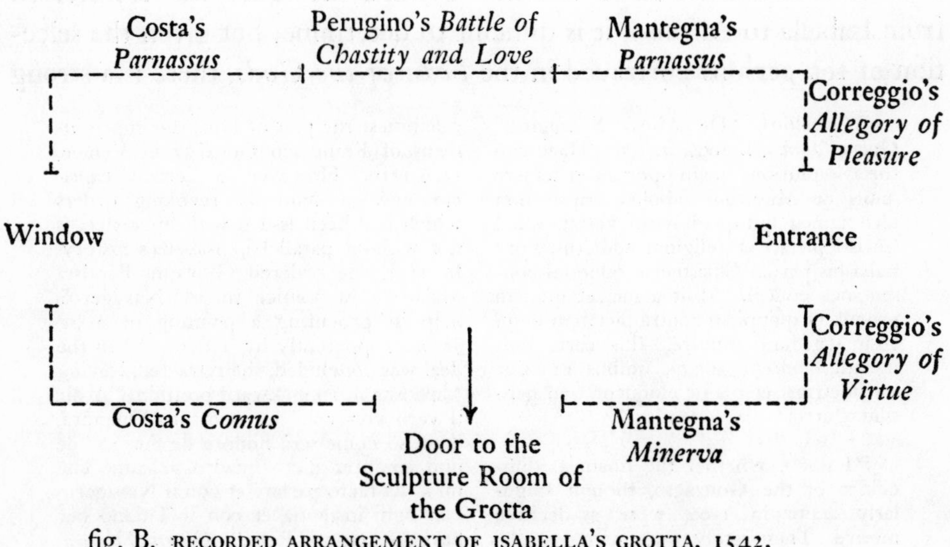

fig. B. RECORDED ARRANGEMENT OF ISABELLA'S GROTTA, 1542.

of Rome.[25] It is difficult to say whether this mood had become Isabella's own with increasing years, or whether she conformed to it as a measure of prudence. Correggio executed the task with such zest that it is impossible to doubt his own sympathy with the assignment; but this may partly be due to his sense of affinity with the admired master of his youth, Mantegna.

If any scruples comparable to those of this late period had prevailed at the time of Isabella's correspondence with Bellini and Bembo, they would easily explain her reluctance to accept Bellini's work when it was finally undertaken; but her convictions at that time were precisely the reverse, as is proved by her own picture of Comus. Her partiality for Costa is a more plausible explanation for her willingness to relinquish her right to Bellini's *Feast of the Gods*. Having employed that jealous but very courteous artist to complete Mantegna's painting of Comus, she may have found it awkward to acquire another and far greater picture of the same kind.[26]

At precisely what stage of Bellini's work the order was transferred from Isabella to Alfonso, it is difficult to determine; but given the selection of the persons portrayed in the *Feast of the Gods*, there is a strong

[25] Gyraldus, "De Musis Syntagma," *Opera Omnia*, I, 1696, p. 568: "Haec ego fortasse pluribus quam oportuit et temere nimis de Musarum fabulis scripsi; non ideo tamen quisquam vitio vertat, quod Christi pietati et religioni addictus, nonnulla his parum Christianae religioni consentanea collegi. Absit a me, et quidem procul, ut quippiam contra pietatem loqui ausim, nedum emutire. Illis certe colligendi laborem ademi, quibus exactior est doctrina, et major eloquentia ad gentilium errores explodendos."

[26] I doubt whether the financial difficulties of the Gonzagas, though singularly acute in 1506, were a decisive motive. They rarely were with Isabella. Of course, there were sufficient other calamities: the pest of 1506, the imprisonment of Francesco Gonzaga in Venice, 1509–1510. However, a certain capriciousness in suddenly revoking orders which had been issued with insistence, is not without parallel in Isabella's history. In 1523, she ordered Giovanni Baptista Malatesta in Venice to ask Navagero's help in procuring a painting of a St. Jerome, apparently by Titian. When the deal was concluded, she retracted, leaving Malatesta in an awkward position: "A dir il vero con voi," he wrote to Calandra, "non so come serà honore de Sua Ex. de non comprar dicto quadro, maxime che mi n' ha facto parlare et con il Navagerio con ogni instantia et con il Titiano per haverlo" (Luzio-Renier, *Giorn. Stor. d. Lett. Ital.*, XXXIV, 1899, p. 48).

probability that the final painting was not begun until after Alfonso had assumed the patronage.[27]

[27] The measurements (1.70 by 1.88 m.) differ slightly from Mantegna's *Parnassus* (1.60 by 1.92 m.) but not sufficiently to exclude the picture *a priori* from Isabella's setting. A. Venturi's suggestion that the so-called *Orpheus* in the National Gallery at Washington, a questionable attribution at best, might be Bellini's *fantasia* for Isabella's studio ("Tre Ignorati Quadri di Giambellino," *L'Arte*, XXIX, 1926, p. 71f.), is contradicted by the size and shape of the picture (0.48 by 0.81 m.).

The Feast of the Gods and Titian's Bacchanals

THE *Feast of the Gods*, no longer wanted for Isabella's Camerino, was among the first pictures to decorate the studio of her brother, Alfonso. We know that Isabella helped him in completing the program, and also that she had cause to regret it; for in December 1515 she made a futile attempt (repeated in March 1516) to recover from him her copy of Philostratus' *Imagines*, a translation which had been made for her by Demetrius Moschus.[1] It was from this book that Alfonso chose the themes of the *Feast of Venus* and the *Bacchanal of the Andrians*, two pictures which Titian executed together with a third representing *Bacchus and Ariadne* (fig. 66–68).[2] Since these three paintings form a perfectly coherent cycle, it is rather surprising that the *Bacchus and Ariadne* should not derive from the same source as the other two.

In the seventeenth century, Ridolfi proposed a theory which has been accepted ever since: that the literary source of Titian's *Bacchus and Ariadne* (fig. 67) is in Catullus, *Carmina* LXIV.[3] There can be little

[1] The translation had a preface by Equicola, in which he recommended the *Imagines* to Isabella as "digne della tua aurea grotta." Quoted by D. Santoro, *Della Vita e delle Opere di Mario Equicola*, p. 64. See also Luzio-Renier, *Giorn. Stor. d. Lett. Ital.*, XXXIII, 1899, p. 22; G. Gronau, "Alfonso d'Este und Tizian," *Jahrbuch der Kunsthistorischen Sammlungen in Wien*, II, 1928, p. 235.

[2] Vasari ("Life of Titian") omits the *Bacchus and Ariadne* from his description of the Titians in Alfonso's chamber. But this must be an error of memory. That the picture hung in one room with the *Bacchanal of the Andrians* is proved by a school drawing in the Santarelli Collection at the Uffizi in Florence, no. 7383, which shows them juxtaposed (illustrated in E. Jacobsen, "Etudes de Titien pour les 'Bacchanales' de Londres et de Madrid," *Gazette des Beaux-Arts*, XXXIX, 1908, p. 135–139).

[3] *Le Maraviglie dell' Arte*, I, p. 142. He may have derived this from G. P. Lomazzo, who had associated this poem

doubt that Titian derived from this poem some of the incidental features of the bacchic procession. The chorus of satyrs and cymbal players might occur in any bacchic scene or poem, but the reference to figures "girt in serpents" (*sese tortis serpentibus incingebant*) is perhaps too precise a parallel to be dismissed. Yet these bacchic accessories are all that the poem and the picture have in common; for Catullus does not describe the actual meeting of Bacchus and Ariadne. On the other hand, the common assumption that the picture represents their first encounter is incompatible with the classical descriptions of that scene, one of which happens to be in Philostratus' *Imagines* (I, 15); for the legend says (and all the classical representations agree on this point) that Bacchus found Ariadne asleep. She did not flee before him, nor did he need to pursue. According to Philostratus, the bacchic revelry was silenced in her presence: "Flowered garments and thyrsi and fawn-skins have been cast aside as out of place for the moment, and the Bacchantes are not clashing their cymbals now, nor are the Satyrs playing the flute, nay, even Pan checks his wild dance that he may not disturb the maiden's sleep."

Obviously Titian's picture does not represent this scene, but a very different encounter between Bacchus and Ariadne, in fact their last meeting before her death, upon his triumphant return from India. And for this the *Fasti* is again the source, as it had been for the *Feast of the Gods*. In explaining the stellar constellation of the "Cnossian Crown," Ovid describes Ariadne's "second despair." Abandoned by Bacchus (as she had been by Theseus), she plaintively walks along the shore, declaiming against the faithlessness of the god and desiring her death. Suddenly she

---

with Bacchic triumphs in general, quoting Titian's *Bacchus and Ariadne*, Bellini's *Feast of the Gods*, and many other examples (*Trattato dell' Arte della Pittura, Scoltura, et Architettura*, 1585, bk. vi, ch. 42, p. 393).

finds herself pursued by Bacchus, who had overheard her prayer as he followed her from behind:

> *Dixerat: audibat iamdudum verba querentis*
> *Liber, ut a tergo forte secutus erat.*[4]

The words *a tergo forte secutus* are superbly rendered by Titian in that pursuing leap of Bacchus, reëvoked in a line of Keats.[5] As Ariadne dies in his embrace, the jewels of her crown are transferred to the sky as a crown of stars. They appear in Titian's painting high above Ariadne, the sign of her apotheosis.[6]

Thus Titian, in a tragic heroic form, resumes the jesting motif of Bellini. The escape from the embrace of the pursuing god is the common theme of both paintings. Whether Bacchus and Ariadne, or Priapus and Vesta, the lovers appear subject to the same law of discord. The rustic couple, in its comic perplexity, foreshadows the grand passion of the heroic pair.

In view of their common source in the *Fasti*, it would seem reasonable to suspect that the painting of Bacchus and Ariadne, though completed later than the scenes from Philostratus,[7] was invented and designed before them; and there is circumstantial evidence to support this conjecture. Though Titian returned from Ferrara in 1516 with the order for a painting on which he began to work at once,[8] it was not until 1518 that he received the program derived from Philostratus. Yet we know that the

[4] *Fasti* III, 505–508.

[5] "Sleep and Poetry": . . . and the swift bound/Of Bacchus from his chariot, when his eye/Made Ariadne's cheek look blushingly.

[6] For classical references to the celestial crown of Ariadne as a symbol of her death (σῆμα ἀποιχομένης 'Αριάδνης) see Pauly-Wissowa, *Realencycl. d. Class. Altertumsw.*, II, 806, *s.v. Ariadne.*

[7] It was seen unfinished in August 1522 by Alfonso's agent in Venice, and not delivered in Ferrara until January 1523 (Crowe and Cavalcaselle, *The Life and Times of Titian*, I, p. 255–258).

[8] Titian's own reference to the first picture ordered by Alfonso as a *bagno* (G. Campori, "Tiziano e gli Estensi," *Nuova Antologia*, XXVII, 1874, p. 585) has baffled all the critics, since no "bath" is known to have been painted for Alfonso by Titian. Is *bagno* perhaps a misreading for *bacco* (possibly spelled *bacho* or even *bagho*)? I hesitate to accept H. Tietze's suggestion that *bagno* is a generic term (*Tizian*, I, p. 160).

subject of the *Feast of Venus* (fig. 66) was chosen by Alfonso at a somewhat earlier date; for there is a drawing of this unusual theme by Fra Bartolommeo (fig. 65), who was employed by Alfonso d'Este and Lucrezia Borgia shortly before his death.[9] Fra Bartolommeo died in 1517; which is the *terminus ante quem* of the drawing. It would seem, therefore, that Alfonso had originally entrusted this theme to him, and that the order was transferred to Titian only after Fra Bartolommeo's death. Had Fra Bartolommeo lived to carry out this work, the role of Bellini as a belated pagan would have been matched in Alfonso's studio by the most pious of Florentines.

In comparing Fra Bartolommeo's sketch with the painting by Titian, it will be found that, with the exception of one single figure, the compositions are independent of each other, Fra Bartolommeo's design being reminiscent of his *Madonna della Misericordia*, in which some forty figures surround the pedestal of the Virgin. Presumably, it was because of his proven competence in handling such a crowded design that Alfonso gave him this particular assignment. The girl offering her mirror to Venus is the only figure which Fra Bartolommeo's sketch has in common with Titian – a subordinate motif in Philostratus, but so prominently stressed in both designs that we may suspect this to be due to Alfonso's explicit instructions.[10] And for these, it is possible to assign a reason. The

[9] H. von der Gabelentz, *Fra Bartolommeo*, I, 1922, p. 131, 198, quotes evidence for Fra Bartolommeo's employment by Alfonso at that period, but does not associate this fact with the drawing of the *Feast of Venus*, the subject of which is left undefined also by B. Berenson, *The Drawings of the Florentine Painters*, II, 1938, p. 31, no. 302, and C. de Tolnay, *History and Technique of Old Master Drawings*, 1943, p. 117, no. 78. E. Jacobsen (*op. cit.*, *Gazette des Beaux-Arts*, 1908, p. 139, n.) realized that the theme was taken from Philostratus, and this was also observed, of course, by Förster, "Wiederherstellung antiker Gemälde durch Künstler der Renaissance," *Jahrb. d. Preuss. Kunstslg.*, XLIII, 1922, p. 126–136. Yet neither of them drew the obvious inference that the sketch must have been part of Fra Bartolommeo's work for Alfonso d'Este, Jacobsen being influenced by the common fallacy that a drawing by Fra Bartolommeo of a pagan subject must antedate his conversion to Savonarola. On this typical error, cf. "Sante Pagnini and Michelangelo: A study of the Succession of Savonarola," Focillon Memorial Volume, *Gazette des Beaux-Arts*, XXVI, published 1947 as of 1944, p. 211–246.

[10] As usual, Alfonso's instructions were

posture of the nymph offering the mirror matches and balances that of the fleeing Ariadne; and again this would seem to imply that the design of *Bacchus and Ariadne* (fig. 67) preceded the design of the *Feast of Venus*, since the posture of Ariadne was determined by the subject, whereas that of the nymph seems superimposed upon the theme and looks somewhat gratuitous even in Titian's version.

And finally, the central Bacchanal itself, representing, as it does, the women of Andros (fig. 68), presupposes the plan of the Ariadne picture; for one of Alfonso's reasons for selecting this rather far-fetched subject from Philostratus — happily not his only reason — seems to have been that *Andriae* is an anagram of *Ariadne*. And again, this would imply that the sequence of invention is irreversible. If the naked woman in the foreground has been taken for an image of the classical Ariadne, the resemblance of posture is not accidental. As an *Andria*, she was meant to suggest Ariadne. Catullus (*Carmina* LXIV, 62) likened the abandoned Ariadne to the image of a bacchante and described her as naked (64–71).

When Titian received the program in 1518, he congratulated Alfonso in a courtly letter on the ingenuity of his "invention," [11] but readers of Philostratus have found it difficult to believe in the sincerity of Titian's applause; for what was there so very ingenious about selecting two descriptions of paintings in Philostratus and asking Titian to follow them to the letter? [12] Yet the felicity with which Titian executed the *Feast of Venus* and the *Bacchanal of the Andrians* leaves no doubt that he was enthusiastic. Actually, there was considerably more to the program than "mere Philostratus"; for in combining these two subjects with the *Bacchus and Ariadne*, Alfonso had devised a sequence which corresponded precisely to the three stages of love in Bembo's *Asolani:* "Chaotic

---

accompanied by a sketch. Cf. letter from his agent, Jacopo Tebaldi, 22 April 1518, Crowe and Cavalcaselle, *op. cit.*, I, p. 182f.

[11] *Ibid.*, p. 181f.

[12] *The Feast of Venus* corresponds to *Imagines* I, 6, the *Andrians* to I, 25 (F. Wickhoff, "Venezianische Bilder," *Jahrb. d. Preuss. Kunstslg.*, XXIII, 1902, p. 118–120).

Love"– "Harmonious Love" – "Transcendent or Divine Love." These were to be illustrated respectively by a bacchanal of children, a bacchanal of adults ("Andrians"), and the bacchanal of the god himself. Hesiod and the Orphics and Plato had asserted (and Ficino and Pico repeated the doctrine) [13] that Love originated in Chaos; and as Love, according to Plato's *Symposium*, was first conceived on the feast of Venus, the picture bearing this title represents the Beginning of Love, the whirlpool of the passions which is Love's infancy. As in Philostratus, this scene is a wild turmoil of cupids shooting at each other with arrows, embracing, wrestling, and playing with apples – the fruit of strife. In the bacchanal of the adults, the apples are replaced by wine, the strife gives way to dance and song, and the wine-inspired music is a well-ordered canon in which the voices resume their theme without end: "Qui boit, et ne reboit, il ne sait que boire soit." [14] As the birth of love is in discord, so the growth of love is in concord; and the consummation of love is a *discordia concors*, a union of both, which is achieved when the mortal is loved by the god himself, but the love of the god means death.

The distance between Bellini's *Feast of the Gods* and the three Bacchanals of Titian is about as great as that between Bembo's *Asolani* and his elegy *Priapus*: the one a fervent, sweeping hymn, written in the vernacular and widely accessible – the other a learned, esoteric caprice, as roguish as it is precious. That these two extremes of Bembo's fancy were represented in the Camerino of Alfonso, shows how much better Bembo was understood in Ferrara, where he had lived for some years, than in Mantua which he visited only as a passing guest. For it remains one of the ironies of this episode that he was able to persuade Bellini on Isabella's behalf, but ultimately failed to persuade Isabella.

[13] Ficino, *In Convivium Platonis De Amore*, I, 3. Pico, *Conclusiones . . . in doctrinam Platonis*, no. 25; also his Commentary on Benivieni's *Canzona d'Amore*, bk. II, ch. 11–14, 19.

[14] Written on the sheet of music, misquoted by Crowe and Cavalcaselle (*op. cit.*, I, p. 228, n.), who also misread *Canon* as *Chanson*. I am indebted for these corrections to Mr. Manfred F. Bukofzer.

In the pleasant competition between brother and sister in the decoration of their Camerini, Alfonso no doubt had incomparable advantages, for the spirit of Bembo was a far greater asset than the bizarre erudition of Paride da Ceresara. Moreover, Alfonso started by acquiring a Bellini which inspired Titian, whereas Isabella began her patronage with Mantegna whose forbidding example discouraged his successors. With the advent of Costa, Isabella's studio was irrevocably on the decline – not even Correggio's genius could counteract the combined dullness of Perugino and Costa – whereas Alfonso's projects reached their fulfillment in the three Bacchanals of Titian.[15]

It was only natural for Titian, once in possession of the full sequence of Alfonso's program, to execute the two paintings from Philostratus first, and conclude with the scene from the *Fasti.* But by then the link with Bellini was broken, and could not be quite restored. In the end the *Feast of the Gods* proved as unsuited for Alfonso's Camerino as it had for Isabella's. The learning of Mantegna dominated the one, Titian's vitality the other. Bellini's gods were strangers in either. In vain Titian tried to amend the misfit by repainting Bellini's background with a heroic landscape, in which his hand has been recognized since the time of Vasari.[16]

[15] What other bacchanalian scenes were in the same room remains a matter of surmise. Vasari mentions a bacchanal by Dosso Dossi ("Life of Girolamo da Carpi") and claims that Dosso's work in the chamber of Alfonso antedated Bellini's *Feast of the Gods* ("Life of Titian"). If these two statements are correct and belong together, the picture cannot be identical with the one recently acquired by the National Gallery in London, which is obviously based on Bellini, repeating his composition in the reverse (fig. 70). The picture even tells the same story, of which it shows an earlier moment, the arrival of Silenus who came to the feast unasked (*Fasti* VI, 324). The crowned female figure in the background could be Cybele (*Fasti* VI, 321). If the picture were hung as a pendant to Bellini's, the symmetry would be so patent as to look hackneyed. Moreover, it is difficult to believe that in a room adorned by pictures with such calculated programs, two pictures would be made to tell the same story. It is more likely that this bacchanal by Dosso was ordered as a free paraphrase of, rather than a pendant to, Bellini's *Feast of the Gods*, and that it was intended for a different setting. Another bacchanal by Dosso, (Castel Sant'Angelo, Rome) has been published by R. Longhi, *Officina Ferrarese*, 1934, p. 141, pl. 189, and is assumed by him to be the one mentioned in Vasari.

[16] "Life of Titian." Vasari accounts for Titian's part in this painting by the

He made the picture look even more hybrid than it did before, and a little top-heavy too, though with an added enchantment; and still it remains a thing apart: for this is essentially a solitary painting – the nostalgic jest of a very old man, conjuring the gods of youth.

For Bembo, too, the painting of this picture must have been inseparable from a nostalgic reflection; for the date coincides with his farewell to the courts of Ferrara, Mantua, and Urbino, where he had been received as *arbiter elegantiae*. When Bellini began to paint the final picture, Bembo was about to exchange the courts for the curia, having been appointed secretary to Leo X. The poetical pagan becoming a cleric and a priest, something of his spiritual withdrawal was paradoxically expressed in the character of the discreet Silenus. It was his last appearance as master of the revels.

---

implausible argument that Bellini was too old and weak to finish it himself, which is contradicted by Bellini's signing and dating the picture and being paid for its completion. Hendy and Goldscheider, *Giovanni Bellini*, p. 30, suggest that Titian may have aimed at bringing "Bellini's picture into better harmony with his own by painting into it a new and looser background." See also Tietze, *Tizian*, I, p. 100. The final answer to this problem will be supplied by Mr. John Walker at the National Gallery on the basis of an X-ray which he was kind enough to let me see. As Mr. Walker intends to deal also with Poussin's copy of the *Feast of the Gods* in Edinburgh, and other copies and paraphrases, I have confined my discussion to Bellini himself and his immediate surroundings.

LIST OF ILLUSTRATIONS

LIST OF ILLUSTRATIONS

with page references to the text

PLATES

1. Giovanni Bellini, The Feast of the Gods. National Gallery, Washington.

2. Giovanni Bellini, Jupiter and the Eagle. Detail of fig. 1.

3. Giovanni Bellini, Neptune and Gaea. Detail of fig. 1.

4. Giovanni Bellini, Nymphs. Detail of fig. 1.

5. Giovanni Bellini, Silenus and Bacchus. Detail of fig. 1.

6. Giovanni Bellini, Priapus and Vesta, Apollo and Ceres. Detail of fig. 1.

7. Niccolò Giolfino, Priapus and Vesta disturbed by the Ass.
John G. Johnson Collection, Philadelphia.

8. Priapus. From Cartari's *Imagini de i Dei degli Antichi*, 1674.

9. Giovanni Bellini, Infant Bacchus. Detail of fig. 1.

10. Unknown Artist, Infant Bacchus. Formerly Benson Collection, London.

11. Giovanni Bellini, Silenus. Detail of fig. 1.

12. Portrait of Pietro Bembo. Engraved by G. Benaglia
after a lost painting formerly in the Nardi Collection, Venice.

13. Valerio Belli, Medal of Pietro Bembo.

14. Portrait of Pietro Bembo.
Mosaic by Francesco and Valerio Zuccato after Titian. Bargello, Florence.

15. Giovanni Bellini, Mercury and Silvanus. Detail of fig. 1.

16. Portrait of Giovanni Bellini.
From Vasari's *Vite*, 1568.

17. Vittore Belliniano, Portrait of Giovanni Bellini.
Musée Condé, Chantilly.

18. Unknown Artist, Medal of Ippolito d'Este.

19. Niccolò Fiorentino, Medal of Alfonso d'Este.

20. Giovanni Bellini, Neptune. Detail of fig. 1.

21. Titian (?), Portrait of Alfonso d'Este. Metropolitan Museum of Art, New York.

22. Paris Bordone, Marriage Painting. Kunsthistorisches Museum, Vienna.

23. Paris Bordone, Marriage Painting. National Gallery, London.

24. Giovanni Bellini, Gaea. Detail of fig. 1.

25. Unknown Artist,
Medal of Lucrezia Borgia.

26. Unknown Artist,
Medal of Lucrezia Borgia.

27. Titian, *Gonfaloniere* Painting for Alfonso d'Este, repainted for Philip II. Prado, Madrid.

28. *Conversione*. From Ripa's *Iconologia*, 1618.

29. Garofalo (?), Minerva and Neptune. Gemäldegalerie, Dresden.

HONOS ET VIRTVS.

ij Cæſaris numiſmati-
rimæ Honoris ac Vir
ıs Virtus ſic eſt expreſ
m pennis ſupra galeã,
ım dextra tenẽs, ocreas
ede teſtudinem, Hono
a eſt expreſſus, intuẽs.
tum, vt fortitudine ad
cet, quo nos ab immi-
ıur. eandemq; ob cauſ-
nnę verò vel criſta, in-
ıt, & ſublimia cogitã-

m vitiorum domandorum, & cupiditatum frenanda-
abent ſignificationem, primùm quòd qui virtutem ſectã

30. *Honos et Virtus.* From Pierio Valeriano's *Hieroglyphica*, 1575.

31. Arbor from Mantegna's Madonna della Vittoria. Louvre, Paris.

32. Arbor in Correggio's Camera di S. Paolo, Parma.

33. Mantegna, Parnassus. Louvre, Paris.

34. Florentine Artist, The Three Graces. Medal of Giovanna Tornabuoni.

35. Mantegna, The Nine Muses. Detail of fig. 33

36. Mantegna, Mars and Venus. Detail of fig. 33.

37. Mantegna, Euterpe and Melpomene. Detail of fig. 33.

38. Mantegna, The Frivolous Muses. Detail of fig. 33.

39. Mantegna, Amor and Vulcan. Detail of fig. 33.

40. Mantegna, Mercury and Pegasus. Detail of fig. 33.

41. Mercury as Horseman. Coin of Antinous.

42. Giovanni dal Cavino, Mercury and Pegasus.
Pseudo-antique Medal of Antinous.

43. *Fama Chiara.* From Ripa's *Iconologia*, 1618.

44. Mantegna, Rabbit and Porcupine. Detail of fig. 33.

45. Pietro da Fano, Amor and Porcupine.
Medal of Lodovico Gonzaga.

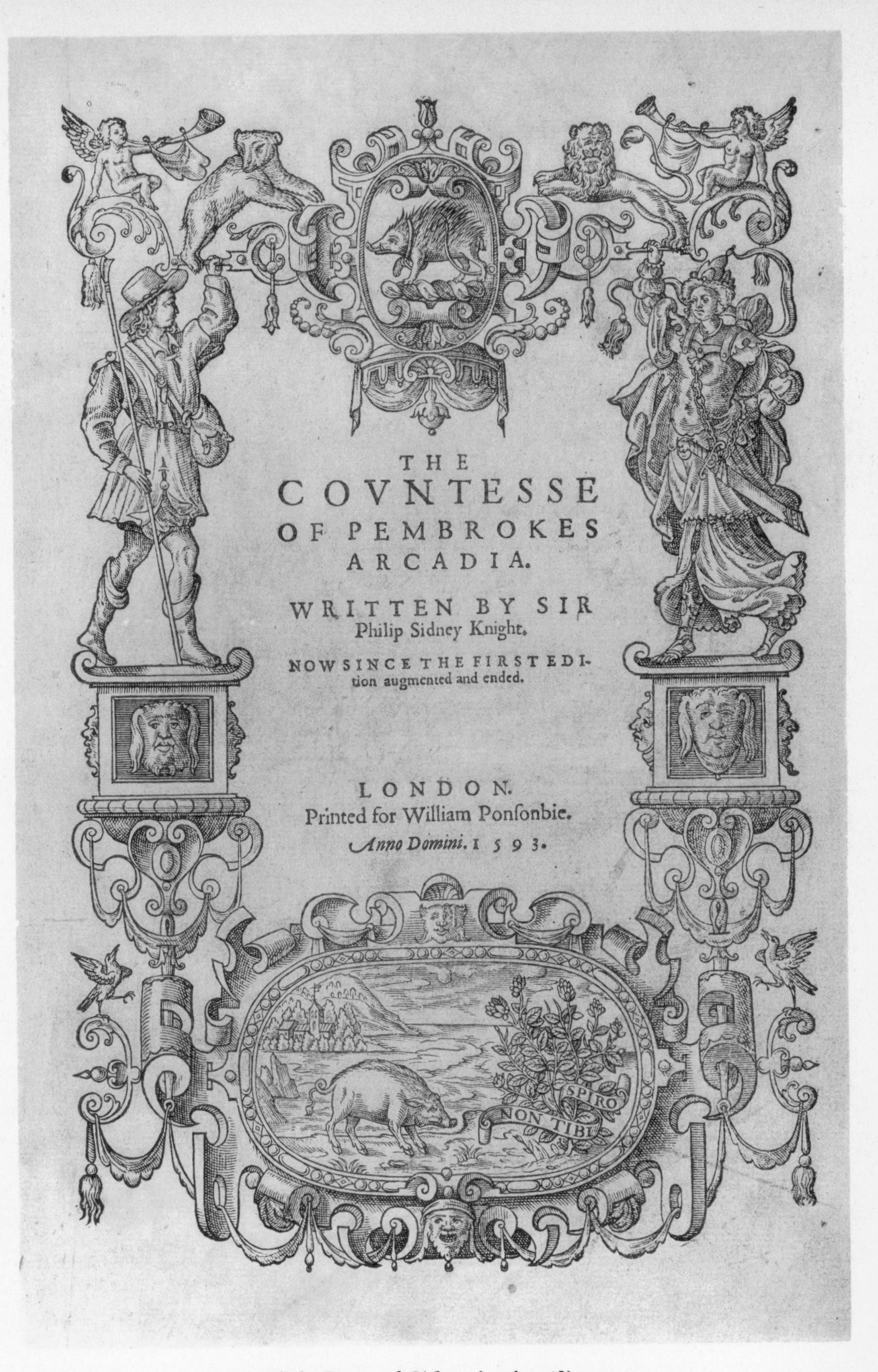
THE
COVNTESSE
OF PEMBROKES
ARCADIA.

WRITTEN BY SIR
Philip Sidney Knight.

NOW SINCE THE FIRST EDI-
tion augmented and ended.

LONDON.
Printed for William Ponſonbie.
Anno Domini. 1593.

46. Title Page of Sidney's *Arcadia*, 1593.

47. School of Mantegna, *Virtus Deserta*. Detail of Engraving.

48. Mantegna, Minerva Expelling the Vices from the Grove of Virtue. Louvre, Paris.

49. Giovanni Bellini, Nemesis. Academy, Venice.

50. Jacopo Bellini, Amor and Fauns. Louvre, Paris.

51. Jacopo Bellini, Triumph of Bacchus. Louvre, Paris.

52. Giovanni Bellini, Mirror (Reconstruction). Academy, Venice.

53. Giovanni Bellini, *Vana Gloria*. Academy, Venice.

54. Giovanni Bellini, *Fortuna Amoris*. Academy, Venice.

55. Giovanni Bellini, *Servitudo Acediae*. Academy, Venice.

56. Giovanni Bellini, *Comes Virtutis.* Academy, Venice.

57. *Bonus Eventus* and Amor as *Comites*.
From Alciati's *Emblemata*, 1542 (Detail).

58. Comus at the Gate. From Cartari's *Imagini de i Dei degli Antichi*, 1580.

59. Lorenzo Costa, The Gate of Comus. Louvre, Paris.

60. The Gate of Comus.
From Vigenère's *Les Images . . . des deux Philostrates*, 1615.

61. Lorenzo Costa, The Garden of Harmony. Louvre, Paris.

62. Perugino, The Battle of Chastity and Love. Louvre, Paris.

63. Correggio, Allegory of Pleasure. Louvre, Paris.

64. Correggio, Allegory of Virtue. Louvre, Paris.

65. Fra Bartolommeo, The Feast of Venus. Uffizi, Florence.

66. Titian, The Feast of Venus. Prado, Madrid.

67. Titian, Bacchus and Ariadne. National Gallery, London.

68. Titian, Bacchanal of the Andrians. Prado, Madrid.

69. Dosso Dossi, Alfonso d'Este as a Bacchic Votary. Brass Collection, Venice.

70. Dosso Dossi, Feast of the Gods. National Gallery, London.

71. Giancristoforo Romano, Medal of Isabella d'Este.

72. Giancristoforo Romano, Medal of Isabella d'Este (chased).
Kunsthistorisches Museum, Vienna.

73. Titian, Portrait of Isabella d'Este. Kunsthistorisches Museum, Vienna.

74. The Muse of History. From a door
in Isabella d'Este's chambers, Palazzo Ducale, Mantua.

INDEXES

BIBLIOGRAPHICAL INDEX OF SOURCES*

Alberti, Leandro, *Descrittione di Tutta Italia*, 1550. (p. 4.)‡

Alciati, Andrea, *Emblematum Liber*, 1531, also 1542. (p. 46, 49, *fig.* 57.)

Arco, Niccolò d', *Numerorum Libri Quattuor*, ed. Z. Betti, with biography by G. M. Mazzuchelli, 1762. (p. 14, 15.)

Bandello, Matteo, *Tutte le Opere*, ed. F. Flora, I, 1934. (p. 15, 17.)

Beccadelli, Antonio, *Hermaphroditus*, ed. F. C. Forberg, 1824. (p. 32.)

[Beccadelli, Lodovico], *Monumenti di Varia Letteratura tratti dai Manoscritti di Monsignor Lodovico Beccadelli*, I, ii, 1799. (p. 21.)

Bembo, Pietro, *Carminum Libellus*, 1552. (p. 28, 31, 61.)

Bembo, Pietro, *De Aetna*, 1495. (p. 21.)

Bembo, Pietro, "De Culice Vergilii et Terentii Fabulis," *Opera*, III, 1567, p. 82–110. (p. 12, 32.)

Bembo, Pietro, *Gli Asolani*, 1505. (p. 22, 27, 60f.)

Bembo, Pietro, *Le Rime*, 1552. (p. 21.)

Bembo, Pietro, *Opere*, Milan, 1808–1810. (p. 42.)

Bembo, Pietro, *Prose nelle quali si ragiona della Volgar Lingua*, 1525. (p. 21.)

Bembo, Pietro, "Sarca," ed. A. Mai, *Spicilegium Romanum*, 1842, p. 489–504. (p. 50.)

Bembo, Pietro, ed., *Le Cose Volgari di Messer Francesco Petrarcha*, 1501. (p. 21.)

Benivieni, Girolamo, "Canzona dello Amor Celeste e Divino, col Commento dello ill. . . . Giovanni Pico Mirandolano," *Opere*, 1522. (p. 11, 61.)

Boccaccio, Giovanni, *Genealogia Deorum*, Paris, 1511. (p. 49.)

Cardanus, Hieronymus, "Liber Duodecim Geniturarum," *Opera*, V, 1663. (p. 15.)

Cartari, Vincenzo, *Le Imagini de i Dei de gli Antichi*, 1580, also 1674. (p. 29, *fig. 8, 58.*)

Cartari, Vincenzo, *I Fasti di Ovidio Tratti alla Lingua Volgare*, 1551. (p. 45.)

Cartari, Vincenzo, *Il Flavio intorno ai Fasti Volgari*, 1553. (p. 45.)

Carteggio Inedito d'Artisti dei Secoli XIV, XV, XVI, ed. G. Gaye, II, 1840. (p. 22, 23.)

Casio de' Medici, Girolamo, *Libro intitulato Cronica, ove si tratta di Epitaphii di Amore et di Virtute*, 1525. (p. 16.)

Castiglione, Baldesar, *Il Cortegiano*, annotato e illustrato da Vittorio Cian, 1929. (p. 22.)

Correggio, Niccolò da, *Opere . . . . intitolate La Psiche e L'Aurora*, 1515. (p. 50.)

Crottus, Aelius Iulius, *Hermione. Eiusdem Floraliorum Spicilegia*, Mantua, 1545. (p. 30.)

* The editions listed are those which were used in this study, not always first editions. Places of publication have been omitted except where title and date would not suffice to identify a book. The list does not include classical authors who might be consulted in any edition. See *Index of Names*. Secondary sources are given in the notes.

‡ Page and figure numbers in parentheses refer to the present book.

Cusa, Nicolaus de, "De Docta Ignorantia," *Opera Omnia*, I, ed. E. Hoffmann and R. Klibansky, 1932. (p. 13.)

Delitiae CC. Italorum Poetarum, ed. Ranutius Gherus [i.e. Janus Gruterus], 1608. (p. 12.)

Diversorum Veterum Poetarum in Priapum Lusus, Venice, 1517. (p. 32, 33, 34.)

Equicola, Mario, *Chronica di Mantua*, 1521. (p. 15.)

Equicola, Mario, *Libro de Natura de Amore*, 1525. (p. 14, 15.)

Equicola, Mario, *Nec Spe Nec Metu*, 1513. (p. 14.)

Erasmus, *Adagiorum Chiliades Tres*, 1508. (p. 46.)

Erasmus, *Colloquiorum Familiarium Opus*, Basle, 1550. (p. 18.)

Erasmus, *Encomium Moriae, i. e. Stultitiae Laus*, Basle, 1515. — Facsimile edition with the marginal drawings of Hans Holbein, intr. H. A. Schmid, tr. H. H. Tanzer, 1931. (p. 7.)

[Erasmus and Morus], *Luciani . . . Opuscula. . . . ab Erasmo Roterodamo et Thoma Moro interpretibus. . . . in Latinorum linguam traducta . . . cum declamatione Erasmica. . . . Declamatio Mori . . .*, 1506. (p. 7.)

Erotopaegnion, sive Priapeia Veterum et Recentiorum [ed. F. J. M. Noël], Paris, 1798. (p. 30.)

Ficino, Marsilio, *Commentarium in Convivium Platonis de Amore*, the text and a translation, with an introduction, by S. R. Jayne, 1944. (p. 11, 61.)

Ficino, Marsilio, *Opera*, 1561. (p. 11.)

Folengus, Theophilus, vulgo Merlinus Cocaius, *Opus Macaronicum*, 1768–1771. (p. 34.)

Gafurius, Franchinus, *De Harmonia Musicorum Instrumentorum*, 1518. (p. 19.)

Gauricus, Lucas, *Tractatus Astrologicus*, 1552. (p. 15.)

Grimaldi, Alessandro, *Oratio Funebris in Funere D. Andreae Alciati*, 1550. — ed. H. Green, 1871. (p. 46.)

Gringore, Pierre, *Les Abus du Monde*, 1509. (p. 13.)

Gyraldus, L. G., "De Musis Syntagma," *Opera Omnia*, I, 1696, p. 555–568. (p. 11, 52ff.)

Gyraldus, L. G., "Historia de Deis Gentium, XVII Syntagmatibus distincta," *Opera Omnia*, I, 1696, p. 1–554. (p. 46, 49.)

Hypnerotomachia Poliphili, 1499. (p. 18, 33, 34.)

[Isabella d'Este], "Carteggio di Isabella d'Este Gonzaga intorno ad un quadro di Giambellino," ed. W. Braghirolli, *Archivio Veneto*, XIII, ii, 1877, p. 370–383. (p. 5.)

[Isabella d'Este], "Notizie di Isabella Estense," ed. C. d'Arco, *Archivio Storico Italiano*, Appendice II, 1845, p. 203–326. (p. 14, 28, 46.)

[Isabella d'Este], "Inventario de li Libri . . . dell' Ill.ma S.ra Isabella d'Este," ed. A. Luzio and R. Renier, *Giornale Storico della Letteratura Italiana*, XLII, 1903, p. 75–81. (p. 45.)

Leone Ebreo, *Dialoghi d'Amore*, ed. S. Caramella, 1929. — *The Philosophy of Love*, tr. F. Friedeberg-Seeley and J. H. Barnes, 1937. (p. 12.)

Lomazzo, Giovanni Paolo, *Trattato dell' Arte della Pittura, Scoltura et Architettura*, 1585. (p. 56f.)

Luciani Opera. Icones Philostrati, Venice, 1503. (p. 47.)

[Mantua], *Delle Arti e degli Artefici di Mantova*, ed. C. d' Arco, 1857. (p. 22, 23, 47.)

[Mantua], "Delle Lettere e delle Arti Mantovane," in S. Bettinelli, *Opere*, XI, 1800, p. 3–196. (p. 15, 16.)

[Mantua], "Della Musica in Mantova: Notizie tratte principalmente dall' Archivio Gonzaga," ed. P. Canal, *Memorie del Reale Istituto Veneto di Scienze, Lettere ed Arti*, XXI, 1879, p. 655–774. (p. 20.)

[Mantua], "Documents inédits tirés des Archives de Mantoue: Documents concernant la personne de messer Pietro Aretino," ed. A. Baschet, *Archivio Storico Italiano*, III, ii, 1866, p. 105–130. (p. 45.)

[Mantua] *La Galleria dei Gonzaga venduta all'Inghilterra nel 1627–28. Documenti degli Archivi di Mantova e Londra*, ed. A. Luzio, 1913. (p. 46, 51.)

[Mantua], "Recherches de Documents d'Art et d'Histoire dans les Archives de Mantoue: Documents inédits concernant la personne et les oeuvres d'Andrea Mantegna," ed. A. Baschet, *Gazette des Beaux-Arts*, XX, 1866, p. 318–339; 478–491. (p. 16.)

Mantuanus, Baptista, *Bucolica seu Adolescentia*, 1498. – *The Eclogues*, ed. W. P. Mustard, 1911. (p. 15.)

Panormita, Antonius, see Beccadelli, Antonio

[Perugino], "Notizie e Documenti inediti intorno a Pietro Vannucci detto il Perugino," ed. W. Braghirolli, *Giornale di Erudizione Artistica*, II, 1873, p. 73–291. (p. 3, 19.)

Pico della Mirandola, Giovanni, *Conclusiones Nongentae in Omni Genere Scientiarum. Adiectum est Panepistemon Angeli Politiani*, 1532. (p. 11, 12, 61.)

Pico della Mirandola, Giovanni – see also: Benivieni, Girolamo, *Canzona dello Amor Celeste e Divino*.

[Pirckheimer], *Podagrae Laus*, appended to: *Luciani. . . . Libellus de non credendo Calumniae*, 1529. – *The Praise of the Gout, or, the Gouts Apologie. . . . written first in the Latin tongue by. . . . B. Pirckheimerus . . . and now Englished by W. Est*, 1617. (p. 7.)

Poggio Bracciolini, "Asinus Luciani. . . . a graeco in Latinum versus"; "Facetiarum Liber," *Opera*, 1538, p. 138–155; 420–491. (p. 7.)

Poliziano, Angelo, "Epistolarum Libri XII," *Opera Omnia*, 1519, fol. 1–122. (p. 12.)

Poliziano, Angelo, "Miscellaneorum Centuria Prima," *Opera Omnia*, 1519, fol. 124v–162. (p. 32.)

Poliziano, Angelo, *Panepistemon*, see Pico della Mirandola, *Conclusiones Nongentae*, 1532. (p. 13.)

Poliziano, Angelo, "Sylvae," *Prose Volgari . . . e Poesie Latine e Grech. . . ,* ed. I. del Lungo, 1867, p. 285–427. (p. 35.)

Raccolta di Lettere sulla Pittura, Scultura ed Architettura, ed. G. Bottari and S. Ticozzi, 1822–1825. (p. 42, 43.)

Ridolfi, Carlo, *Le Maraviglie dell'Arte*, 1648. – ed. D. von Hadeln, 1914–1924. (p. 21, 56.)

Ripa, Cesare, *Iconologia*, 1618. (p. 11, 12, 20, 37, 38, *fig. 28, 43*.)

Sanuto, Marino, *I Diarii*, IV, 1880. (p. 28.)
Sidney, Sir Philip, *The Countesse of Pembrokes Arcadia*, 1593. (p. 13, *fig. 46*.)
Spagnolo, Baptista, see Mantuanus, Baptista

Toscano, Raffaello, *L'Edificatione di Mantova*, Padua, 1586. (p. 4.)
Trissino, Giovan Giorgio, *La Sophonisba, Li R[i]tratti. . .*, 1549. (p. 4, 51.)

Valeriano, Pierio, *Hieroglyphica*, 1575. (p. 39, 49, *fig. 30*.)
Vasari, Giorgio, *Le Vite de' più eccellenti Pittori, Scultori, e Architettori*, 1568. — ed. G. Milanesi, 1878–1885. (p. 16, 21, 38, 42, 43, 56, 62, *fig. 16*.)
Vigenère, Blaise de, tr., *Les Images ou Tableaux de Platte Peinture des deux Philostrates, enrichis d'arguments et annotations*, 1615. (p. 47, *fig. 60*.)

INDEX OF NAMES

THIS BOOK HAS BEEN PRINTED BY THE
HARVARD UNIVERSITY PRINTING OFFICE FOR THE
DEPARTMENT OF PRINTING AND GRAPHIC ARTS
IN THE HARVARD COLLEGE LIBRARY

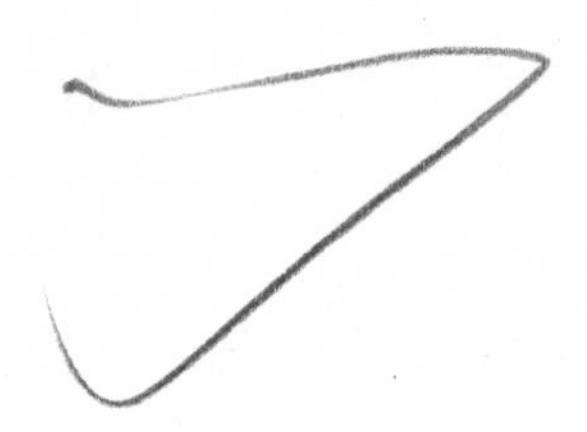